Sweet Scent of Justice

Sweet Scent of Justice

A FAITH-BASED, TRUE CRIME MEMOIR

By

Debbie Wilson

Unless otherwise indicated, all Scripture quotations are taken from The Living Bible copyright © 1971. Used by permission of Tyndale House Publishers, Inc., Carol Stream, Illinois 60188. All rights reserved.

Front cover design by Bradley Wind

Author pictures by Margie Nielsen Photography

Newspaper photo by Mark Rainwater

All other photos from the author's collection

Copyright © 2012

ISBN: 0985553200

ISBN 13: 9780985553203

Dedications

To my beautiful sister, Kathy. I miss you every day!

To my two daughters, three nieces, and three nephews who never knew their Aunt Kathy. My hope is you will catch a glimpse of the beautiful person she was and learn the importance of faith and forgiveness.

To Royce Toney, Major Richard Medaries, Trooper Todd Cummings, and the entire Ouachita Parish Sheriff's

Office for your hard work and determination to solve Kathy's cold case.

To District Attorney Jerry L. Jones and Assistant District Attorney Stephen Sylvester for your professionalism and passion to see justice prevail.

To the members of the Vidocq Society for using your valuable resources and time to move Kathy's case forward.

Contents

"A strong woman knows she has enough strength for the journey, but a woman of strength knows it is in the journey where she will become strong."
-Unknown

Author's Note

Everything I have written in *Sweet Scent of Justice* is true; it contains the memories I have of all the events that took place before and after my sister's murder. Newspaper articles containing facts from the crime, notes from interviews, official trial transcripts, and conversations were also used to give accurate information to my account. Quotations and dialogue are written for effect to capture the essence of what was said and are not necessarily the exact words of the speaker. To protect the privacy of others, some names have been changed.

Sweet Scent of Justice

Introduction
(A Diamond in the Rough)

*W*hen my two daughters were young, my husband and I took them on vacation with some good friends to a diamond mine in Arkansas; we spent a whole day in the sweltering heat looking for diamonds. I had never been to a diamond mine before, so I was surprised when we saw what appeared to be an enormous garden filled with rows and rows of freshly plowed dirt. We arrived armed with our little shovels and started digging right away in the hot, July sun. We dug around in the dirt for hours only to find several huge spiders but not one single diamond.

As we were leaving, I caught a glimpse of a picture on the wall in the Visitors' Center of the last diamond that had been found in the mine. I turned back and walked closer. I couldn't believe what I was seeing. The diamond looked like a dirty, yellow rock. Hanging right above the picture was the inscription: "Diamond in the Rough."

I could have very well thrown away several real diamonds worth millions during my hours of searching because I wasn't looking for something that at all resembled the gem in the picture. I didn't understand that a diamond in the rough is not shiny and beautiful when it is first formed. It is only after it has been cut with precision many times by a jeweler that it begins to reflect the light that gives it its beauty.

For seventeen years, I was just like that diamond in the rough; my life was free of any major pain or sorrow, free from any cuts that life can inflict upon a person. Even though I went to church every time the doors were open, and I knew I was a Christian, my faith had never really been tested. Then on April 4, 1981, one month before I graduated from high school, I experienced a deep cut that would not only test my faith, it would change my life and the lives of my family forever.

....

Chapter 1

Saying Goodbye

remember Amy washing dishes and banging pots and pans as she stuffed them in the cabinets. Then she started on the countertops, wiping the surface over and over in circles as fast as she could. At thirteen, she usually never cleaned, but that morning was different. Steve played in our game room sticking Legos together in no meaningful shape. At eight, he was a master of Lego design, but that morning he couldn't seem to form his usual masterpieces. At eighteen, I sat on the end of the couch in the den, in charge of the kids and flipping cards, thinking I was playing solitaire but not really paying attention to what I was doing. I just needed my hands to be moving, so I could be doing something other than sitting still and waiting for Daddy and Mama to get back from the twenty-mile trek to the police station.

I can't think of many things that could get me up at six on a Saturday morning other than this one thing— the finding of a little blue mustang with keys in the ignition, purse on the passenger seat, and no sister.

I have never played solitaire again since that day.

∽

In 1981, our house was the "go-to spot" for fun-filled Friday nights, watching movies till dawn, baking blueberry muffins, playing cards, and just acting crazy with my older sister, Kathy, and our church's youth group. But this particular Friday night in April, she promised to spend the night with two new friends from her workplace, where she was a part-time secretary.

She had just gotten home from work when I saw her packing and complaining, mostly about staying with the two girls. They had asked her many times to visit with them on the weekend, but she always made an excuse. She just didn't know them very well, and she grew tired of making up excuses, so tonight was the night.

Kathy was the type of person who wouldn't hurt anyone's feelings in a million years if she could help it. Besides, she loved to be around lots of people. She would occasionally hang out with friends at college clubs, even though she didn't drink alcohol, just so she could meet new people and dance. I guess that's one reason she agreed to spend the night with the two girls from work. They were all going to go hang out at a club, so she decided the night wouldn't be too bad after all.

Early that Friday evening, Kathy took a shower and went upstairs to her room to get ready. I stayed downstairs in the hall bathroom curling my hair, getting ready for my date with my high school sweetheart, Todd. I had known him since kindergarten, and we'd been dating steadily for the whole four years of high school. In a couple of hours, we'd be watching the next episode of *Dallas* and eating pizza as we cuddled up together on our couch in the game room.

My primping was interrupted when I heard the phone ring. I put down the curling iron and went to Mama's room to answer it.

"Hello?"

"Hello...Is Kathy home? Can I speak to her please?"

I knew all of Kathy's friends, but I didn't recognize this girl's voice at all. I screamed up the stairway for Kathy to get the phone. I hung up when I heard her pick up the receiver at the top of the stairs and went back to curling my hair.

When I heard Kathy come running down the stairs, I walked into the den and asked, "Who called?"

She gave me a wrinkled-nose look and said, "That was Jessie's new girlfriend."

Jessie was a guy Kathy had dated steadily for many months while she was in high school before the relationship finally ended.

"Why was she calling you?"

"She said she wanted to meet with me to talk about Jessie."

Kathy walked right past me and headed down the hall as if she were looking for something.

"Are you going to meet her?" I shouted after her.

"No! I'm not about to get myself in the middle of something that's between the two of them," she shouted back.

She really didn't go into any more of the details of their conversation, but I knew she had no intention of meeting with her, and we both thought it was a rather strange phone call. After all, Kathy was glad to finally get out of the relationship. She still cared deeply for the guy, and they were friends; but the relationship was over, and she was already dating someone else— one of the guys from our youth group.

I went back into the hall bathroom to finish curling my hair, and she headed back upstairs. I was so interested in getting ready for my date with Todd that I didn't think any more about the call.

Todd would be arriving soon, and I had one last finishing touch waiting to be found, somewhere. I searched frantically for my gold-stretch belt that I knew would complete my outfit. After finding it, I walked into the den with belt in hand; Kathy stood by the couch looking so pretty in her blue jeans and black button-up shirt. She had on the gold necklace and earrings that she always wore, and the curls of her beautiful strawberry-blonde hair touched her shoulders so perfectly.

The scent of lavender followed her and her little blue overnight case around the living room. Glancing back to see me putting on my belt, she did an about face.

"Hey, let me borrow that belt."

"Why? Where's yours?" I asked.

"I can't find mine. I'm in a hurry. Let me have it."

"I don't think so. I'm wearing it."

"Why do you even need a belt? You and Todd are just going to stay home and watch TV. You're not even going out anywhere. Please!"

"No, it's mine, and I'm wearing it. Find your own belt!"

"I'm going out dancing tonight. Please let me wear it! I'm begging you!"

"I said No!"

Kathy and I rarely argued, but on that particular night, I got my way and she got mad. Still, she didn't forget to stop at the kitchen table to leave a note for Mama with the names and phone numbers of the girls she would be staying with that night, so Mama could call if she needed her. With that last responsibility taken care of, she got into her little blue Mustang, and that was the last I saw of her.

(Kathy's little blue Mustang)

❧ *Chapter 2* ❧

....

Unwelcome News

$\mathcal{I}$m sure Daddy and Mama were worried, but they tried not to show it as they woke up Amy, Steve, and me early the next morning. They woke up my grandparents too. My mother's parents, Papaw and Mamaw, lived right beside us in a house that was almost identical to ours. Daddy had taken mechanical drawing classes in college, so he drew up the plans for the two houses; when I was about two years old, Daddy and Papaw built both homes with some help from a local contractor.

Being so close, Papaw and Mamaw spent just as much time with us growing up as Daddy and Mama did. They were like second parents to us; and since Mama worked full time, even in the summers, Mamaw watched all four of us from the time we were born until we were old enough to go to school.

Picture of my grandparents' house

(Left to right: Debbie, Daddy, and Kathy)

During the twenty-mile drive to the police station, I'm sure Daddy tried to think of a logical reason why Kathy would just abandon her car. If I had to describe Daddy in just one word it would be "logical." As a matter of fact, my family had even given him the nickname, "Logical Lee Roy" because of his gifted way of reasoning things out and making sense of every situation. I guess that's what made him such a good math and science teacher. His logical nature usually kept him calm and collected, except for that one time with the car and the tractor and me.

I remember Kathy pleading my case to let me practice driving: "I'll make sure she takes her time and drives slowly," Kathy assured him. "I'll be sitting on the front seat right beside her. I'll even drive the Cutlass to the backyard myself before I let her get behind the wheel." Kathy was two years older than me, and she had already been driving for a few years. After hearing an earful of our pleading, Daddy approved our request.

Our house sat on three acres of land, and most of the yard was cleared off with the exception of a line of pine trees at the far end of the property that marked a lower area of ground. Before handing me the keys, Daddy made me promise that I wouldn't go past that line of trees at the very back of the yard because it had rained the day before, and he thought we might get the car stuck.

After making several loops around the backyard with Air Supply booming in our ears from the eight-track-tape player, Kathy turned down the music and looked at me: "You know," she said, "you're going to have to parallel park when you go take your driving test."

"I am?"

"Yep! Let's practice. Try to parallel park between those two pine trees." She pointed to the line of trees Daddy had told us to stay away from.

"I better not do that. That's where Daddy said not to go."

"He said we couldn't go past the trees. He didn't say anything about going between them. It will be fine. Trust me!"

I always erred on the side of caution, but Kathy was just the opposite. She had an independent nature, and I admired that quality in my big sister.

I pulled the car up so that the back of the car was even with one of the trees, and then I turned the wheel as I slowly backed the car up and fit it perfectly between the two pines. I grinned proudly and said, "I think I did that even better than you could have done it!" At that moment I felt my heart sink with the tires as they dipped into the wet dirt. We both looked at each other with wide eyes.

Kathy said, "You better go get Daddy."

We walked up to the house and met Daddy under the carport. There, I told him what I had done. And I waited. In a brief moment, a bright shade of red glowed on his disgusted, furrowed face. Shaking his head back and forth, he calmly said, "I'll go get the tractor at Papaw's and pull you out."

On his way to get the tractor, I'm sure he tried to reason out why we would think that it was a good idea to wedge the car between the two trees. It was that thinking nature that kept him from yelling.

God had also gifted Daddy with another nature. Most people joked he had to be a kin to Job (from the book of Job in the Bible) because he had such an abundance of patience. That day, though, I sensed we wore his patience thin.

Daddy pulled the tractor around and attached a chain from the hitch to the front bumper of the car. Smoke bellowed from the exhaust pipe as he pulled on the car several times trying to free it from the mud, but just when he thought the tires were loosening from the wet dirt, the tractor sank and became stuck too. That's when he raised his voice and yelled, "Confound it, Debbie! I asked you not to drive down here!" That was the first and only time I ever remember Daddy yelling at me.

I flipped a king of spades over and wished I could hear him yelling now, all the way from the police station, to tell me where my sister was. Without cell phones, the only thing I could do was wait.

❦

The back door banged the wall as it flew open and swung back. Mama stood motionless in the kitchen, tears streaming down her swollen face; Daddy's thin lips pressed so tightly together that his eyes were almost completely closed; his face had a strange red hue all over—a look of sadness I'll never forget as long as I live.

I stopped the endless card flipping and jumped up to meet them. Daddy rushed into the den and held my arm as he led me back toward the couch. Amy and Steve followed us. Through Mama's weeping Daddy took a deep breath before saying those words, those deafening words: "Kathy's gone. Someone shot her."

My legs crumbled underneath me as if they had no muscle in them at all. I fell to the floor, sobbing uncontrollably.

Time stopped.

It just stood still.

So many what ifs and whys and how comes went through my mind in just a few seconds that I felt dizzy and disoriented. I didn't know how to respond; I never studied about this in school, so I kept asking myself, *What do I do? How am I supposed to act?* I had only seen such tragedies on television.

I had never felt grief or pain like the pain I felt at that moment.

I knew enough about God, though, to cry out to Him, asking Him to wake me up from the nightmare. Within moments, my grief gave way to rage. I grabbed one of the end-table legs next to the couch and tried to rip it off. I pulled on it as hard as I could and tried to snap it into a million pieces. Daddy picked me up off the floor and helped me to the couch. I pressed my face deeply into his chest while he wrapped his arms around me. His wet tears fell on mine as he held me tighter than he had ever held me before. I had always felt safe and secure in my daddy's arms, but this time the hurt I felt was too deep to be comforted, even by him.

My thoughts became consumed with our last words together:

"I'm going out dancing tonight. Please let me wear it! I'm begging you!"

"I said NO!"

I thought about how she begged me to let her wear my gold belt, and I wouldn't let her. I thought about how she really didn't want to stay with the girls from work, but she had turned them down so many times before that she felt guilty, so she accepted their invitation. I was so angry at her for not giving them another excuse and staying home that night.

Between his tears my baby brother gave us some relief from the torment, if we chose to accept it: "Well, she's in heaven," he said with a wet but confident look. "She's with Jesus. Right?"

Intellectually, I knew he was right because when Kathy was just a young girl, maybe Steve's age, she had asked Jesus to forgive her of her sins and to be the Lord of her life. At that moment, she had been given the free gift of salvation, of eternal life with God. But even that fact could not comfort me.

Within minutes of my parents' arrival, Papaw and Mamaw ran across the well-worn path that started at their back door and seemed to end in our living room: "What's the matter? What's wrong?" Mamaw asked, gasping for breath.

What else could Daddy say, but "She's dead. Kathy's dead. She was shot to death."

Mamaw dropped to her knees on the kitchen floor and screamed, "Why did he have to kill her? I knew that boy was going to kill her." Papaw just held her, and we all sat together in unified shock.

Daddy got up and walked over to the phone to call our pastor. He needed his friend and minister to come pray with us. He called others, and they called others. Daddy's friend and co-worker, "Hawk," arrived first. I can still hear all the knocks on the back door and the ringing of the doorbell as people arrived.

Before long, a flock of friends and relatives crowded into the house. I looked across the crowd and thought there had been a huge mistake and at any moment Kathy would walk through the back door smiling and making jokes about all the company. But I knew it wouldn't happen. I sat on the couch wondering, *Why is this happening to us? This is not supposed to happen to good people—not to people who love the Lord and try to live for Him.* To my surprise, an answer came, like someone had slipped my mind a long-lost note with a verse from Psalm 56 written on it: "What time I am afraid, I will trust in thee." When I was a little girl, I would repeat that verse over and over if I went into a dark room or if I got lost from Mama in a store. In that moment, I surely was afraid; the only blanket of comfort I could wrap around my heart was the promise I had always been told about—that I could trust my Father in heaven, who now shared His presence with Kathy.

It seems so strange to me that when I try to remember the details of April 4, 1981, I vividly see and hear everything I have just written, as though it happened an hour ago; but the hours, days, weeks, and even

months after that day are overshadowed by an indescribable cloud of darkness. The cloud hovered over
my family and me while we inched our way through
the stages of grief I would later read about in my college psychology classes. We all lost a year of our lives
just trying to make it through one day at a time. I
tried to rely only on God to help me get through each
minute of every day.

෨

It seemed so easy before Kathy was killed to tell
everyone how much faith I had in God. After all, my
days were so carefree during my senior year of high
school. I worked at a local department store so I could
make enough money to buy the latest fashions to wear
for my dates with Todd. We spent all of Friday and
Saturday together. And since we attended the same
church, we spent Sundays together too.

With a month left to graduate high school, we had
been dating for over four years, and I had no desire
to look for romance with anyone else. The only con-
cern I had in the world was that my final term paper
would soon be due in English. I had procrastinated for
too long on writing the paper, and I knew this meant

I would have to give up some time with Todd that weekend to work on it.

In the fall, I would attend the nearby university where Kathy went to school as a business major and take courses in elementary education. My desire to be a teacher came from Daddy, who had taught math and science for many years before becoming the principal at my own high school. While most teenagers would cringe at that very thought, I delighted in the fact that I could count on him to be near me, to protect me and talk to me.

The desire to work in education came from Mama too, who had gone to work right out of high school as the secretary for the school district's superintendent and had worked there for over twenty years. With all this influence, becoming an educator was my childhood dream. I even played school as a little girl with Kathy and our best friends, Carol and Lori.

Of course, the plan would be tied with a perfect bow when I married Todd after college. We talked about marriage and kids and family vacations many nights as we sat in the swing in my backyard or rode around the rural Louisiana countryside in his four-wheel-drive truck listening to Journey or our favorite song, "Endless Love."

But now I realized how naïve I had been. Some loves do end. I wondered what else wasn't true—what about the songs in church? What about my favorite verses in the Bible that I kept repeating over and over again, like:

> *Psalm 55:22: "Give your burdens to the Lord. He will carry them."*
>
> *Psalm 9:9: "All who are oppressed may come to Him. He is a refuge for them in their time of trouble."*
>
> *Romans 8:28 (KJV): "And we know that all things work together for good to them that love God, to them who are called according to His purpose."*
>
> *Philippians 4:13 (KJV): "I can do all things through Christ who strengthens me."*

Even though my mind sometimes debated with my soul over their truth, every spark of God's Spirit within me said they were real and alive for me as I went through my pain. I repeated these scriptures in the shower, in the car, and in my bed day and night. I needed to remind myself that even though it seemed like my whole world was crashing down around me, God was still with me, and He was still in control. I believed this in my heart, but I would eventually have to go back to high school and try to act as if my life wasn't in shambles.

❧ Chapter 3 ❧

....

Back to Reality

"It's almost time to go," Mama yelled through the open sliding glass door in the den. "Come inside and get ready," she shouted, calling out to Steve several times before he came running to the door, looked at her with tears in his eyes, and said, "I just want to stay here, Mama, and play ball as hard as I can, so I don't have to think."

An eight-year-old little boy expressed exactly what we were all feeling. We didn't want to have to think any more either about the fact that Kathy was dead or about the horrible events she had been through or how we were about to bury her.

Mama let Steve stay at the house with friends and family and didn't push him to go with us the night of visitation. I wanted desperately to stay home with him, and I wanted all the people in the house to just go away. I know that sounds ungrateful, but I wanted things to return to normal, and how could they if all those people were still there.

As we arrived at the church the next day for the funeral, the parking lot had already filled. The funeral assistant motioned for Daddy to pull the car directly behind the hearse near the front doors of the church. Mama sniffled as she peered into the back glass knowing that her first-born child's coffin would soon be placed into it.

Daddy and Mama led us through the church to the front pew; each stare felt like a knife piercing my chest. Every pew in our rather large church was filled to capacity, and people were standing in the aisles and along the back wall. Our entire community wanted to pay their respects to Kathy and our family. I wanted desperately to disappear.

Kathy's casket sat right in front of us, and I was so thankful that Daddy and Mama had chosen to keep it closed through the funeral. I don't remember any-thing about the service because the whole time I just sat there praying that it would hurry up and end. I thought if it would just end, the nightmare I had been living in might end, too.

After the service, the funeral procession made its way to the cemetery. The pallbearers lifted her shiny, gray casket from the hearse and carried it to her final resting place. The pastor's words reminded us that Kathy was no longer with us because she was in her eternal home with Jesus.

I knew that he was right and when I found Kathy's autobiography, which she had written just a few months before the murder, it confirmed the pastor's words. She wrote:

Life for all of us is filled with experiences, relationships, emotions, triumphs, and sorrows. Throughout our lives we are all influenced by people and happenings around us. Some of the most memorable times of my life have been spent with my family. My family is very important to me. They have shared my happy times and have helped me through the bad. No matter what, I feel secure knowing they will always stand behind me and be supportive in all that I do.

The most important part of my being is the fact that I am a Christian. To me, that's what life is all about. Ever since I can remember I have gone to church regularly with my parents. The fact that they are

Christians has influenced and set a pattern for me. I accepted Christ into my life when I was nine years old, and since then the Lord has been number one in my life. I feel that God has a special plan for my life. Today the world is filled with so called "Sunday Christians," people who only seem to be religious on Sundays. True Christians should live their lives for Christ every day. Thinking about my future is sort of scary. I have quite a few decisions to make before I finish college. My hope for the future is that I will be a success at whatever I decide to do. It is extremely important to me that I strive to reach my goals.

I just thank the Lord for the happy memories of my life so far.

I tried to imagine Kathy in heaven, but even that didn't heal the fresh, open wounds bleeding with sorrow.

Walking into the house after leaving the cemetery, I could barely tolerate the aroma of casseroles and cakes that had been prepared for us while we were at the church. My stomach stayed tied in knots after our long morning of grief. I tried to eat, but couldn't. I felt claustrophobic and found it hard to breathe. I went to my room.

❧

Daddy and I rode to school together our first day back. The silence was deafening, but what could we say? We both knew we were about to go back to the school we had left when our lives were in a perfect place, a wonderful place. Now we were returning to a completely different reality. My stomach felt sick, knotted tighter by nerves. Now I knew exactly how Kathy felt during junior high. Before morphing into our strong-willed, social butterfly, she cried every day from the social pains of shyness, wondering how she would make friends. Almost every day, she called Mama who worked across the street to come and pick her up. I cried, too, that day as we made the drive, knowing I would have to face a whole school full of curious students who heard about her death and would certainly stare. I dreaded those stares most of all and silently wished Mama would come to pick me up too.

Homicide in a community of 14,000 people is always big news; the whole city buzzed about who might have killed a nineteen-year old college sophomore and why. Many of the details of her death were not released until several weeks after her murder, so my friends kept asking me specific questions like:

"Was she killed next to her car on the rural road?"

"Where was her body found?"

I felt almost ashamed because I really didn't have all the answers to their questions. One of my friends even asked me if Kathy had been raped. Daddy and Mama never said anything about rape, so I let her know in no uncertain terms that she had not been raped, even though I really didn't know if she had been or not.

I know everyone just tried to be supportive, but I wanted to pretend Kathy's death had never happened, at least during the school day. I didn't want to talk about what happened to my sister. I wanted a break from a house that felt empty and a family that seemed incomplete.

There were many times I passed by Daddy's office during the day, but he wasn't where he normally sat behind his desk. I just wanted to see his face and hear him ask, "What's up, Deb? How's your day going?"

Instead, I saw an empty chair that made me feel even emptier.

Many years later, he told me he left the school during the day to drive to the cemetery. He would stand by Kathy's graveside so he could be close to her. He knew that it was only her casket beneath the ground and her soul was in heaven, but he just needed a private place to grieve.

All the buzz in the community and on the news led to rumors that her ex-boyfriend or her friends from work had something to do with the murder. This talk eventually filtered its way down to Amy's junior high school, a place where young teens are less compassionate than high school students about how they ask questions; they didn't really care if they hurt her feelings. Amy's friends tried to shield her from it, but the intense questioning during the final days before summer break became more and more painful for her.

Since Steve was only in the third grade, he escaped the questions that Amy and I faced daily, but his grades plummeted. Daddy and Mama usually supported him with his lessons; but now, they were only strong enough to offer us support from the tragedy.

How we ate, slept, worked, and played as a family changed, too. A few years before Kathy's death, Daddy added an upstairs addition to the house; and because we were the oldest, Kathy and I got to stay in the two new bedrooms. How thrilled we were to have our own private space together, yet still separate.

After Kathy died, I had no desire to go upstairs. My brown bedspread, curtains, and carpet that once comforted me with their neutrality were now dark and depressing. I didn't want to pass by Kathy's room either, expecting to see her sitting in front of her vanity, hand-made by Daddy, or on her pretty blue-and-white lace comforter sorting pictures to post on her cork board. Even the lightness of her matching curtains and carpeting she picked out became a morbid hue. So

I moved into Amy's room with her, which was right beside Steve's room and across the hall from Daddy and Mama. I knew I no longer lived in the same innocent world I had lived in all my life. I now wanted to stay as close as I could to Daddy and Mama.

No matter how hard we tried to move on with our lives during the first year after her death, the memories kept hurting us, so we kept trying different ways to create new memories; we changed the traditions of Christmas and other holidays. Instead of opening presents upstairs at Mamaw's house, like we used to, we stayed downstairs in the living room. We even moved our favorite family vacation spot from Panama City, Florida to Gulf Shores, Alabama. But it didn't matter how deep or how far we tried to tuck away our memories of Kathy, the pain just wouldn't go away.

A lady at the funeral, who had also experienced a tremendous loss when her husband unexpectedly died, approached Mama. She said that time would be the only thing that would help heal the hurt. That's when I began praying for God to speed up time so my hurt would be less painful.

The lady was right; the pain did ease over time and with God's help. From time to time over the years, Kathy's name would be mentioned on the news or in the newspaper when something new developed in her unsolved case, but life went on. We rarely mentioned her name or spoke about her when our family was together. We had sent Kathy to her own room in our private memories.

৵৹

Some things in my life still worked out as planned. In the fall, I enrolled in the same university where Kathy had attended, and in 1985, earned a degree in elementary education. After graduation, I married Todd and started teaching fourth grade at a local elementary school. Six years later, our family began with the birth of our first daughter, Brittany.

On the day of her birth, a large crowd of family and friends peered into the nursery awaiting her arrival. Brittany's Uncle Steve and Aunt Amy welcomed their first niece into the world, but how I wished with all my heart that her Aunt Kathy could have been there too.

Twelve months later, Todd and I spent many nights searching through hundreds of baby names trying to decide on a name for our next baby girl. When she arrived, it seemed natural to call her Katelyn, after Kathy.

The girls sometimes saw me crying on Kathy's birthday or the anniversary of her death; so when they were old enough to understand, I told them about their Aunt Kathy, how much I missed my sister, but I only gave them bits and pieces of information about her death. The older they got, the more frequently and intensely came their questions, especially during their early teens. They asked questions like,

"How did Aunt Kathy die, Mama?"

"Who killed her?"

"Why would somebody want to hurt her?"

I always tried to change the subject, just like I had done every day at high school or in the grocery store when someone asked me about Kathy's death. I became quite efficient at finding ways to avoid those memories, so it wasn't difficult at all for me to do the same with my own daughters.

As older teenagers, though, the questions came even more frequently. During one round of interrogation, I became very frustrated with Brittany and blurted out, "I don't really know what happened to Kathy!"

With wide eyes and exasperation in her voice, she said, "Why don't you know, Mama? She was your sister."

Her words hit me like a truckload of bricks. I felt such guilt. I had achieved all the goals of my five-year plan, but I knew in my heart that my plan would have been much more complete if I had been able to share each milestone with my big sister. I owed it to her to find out who shot her and why.

❧ Chapter 4 ❧

....

Start of a Journey

Some people go through a type of midlife crisis when they turn forty. The year I turned forty, I began a journey to end a crisis.

A few weeks before my fortieth birthday, in October of 2003, an overwhelming desire to reopen an old chapter in my life filled my inner being—the chapter of Kathy's unsolved murder. I covered the pain of that crisis for so long that I didn't even know how to start opening it. At first, I thought the anxiety I felt was just about turning forty, but the desire to learn all I could about the murder gripped my heart and wouldn't let go.

I kept the desire quiet at first. After all, for over twenty-two years, my family hadn't even mentioned Kathy's name much because talking about her only brought back unbearable thoughts. No pictures of Kathy were hung in the house, except for the family portrait taken only months before she was killed. Mama moved that picture to the back hall a few months after her death, so she wouldn't have to see it every day. We certainly had not forgotten about her, especially on her birthday or the anniversary of her death—we just didn't talk about her—it was too painful.

No matter how hard I tried, I couldn't put the desire to find out exactly what happened to Kathy behind me. I couldn't rest at night. I couldn't get her off of my mind. I wanted to find answers to the questions the girls had always asked throughout the years. I wanted to know the whole story from beginning to end, no matter how painful that story might be. I didn't want to spend any more of my life trying to block out that awful day.

Her death weighed heavily on my mind that October. I wanted answers, so I asked God, who I believed put this desire in me (it was just an unexplainable sense of His hand on my heart), *Okay, Lord, how do I start or even continue an investigation that the police closed long ago?*

Our family portrait taken a few months before Kathy was killed.

(Front row-Left to right: Kathy, Mama, Steve, and me)
(Back row-Left to right: Amy and Daddy)

❧ Chapter 5 ❧

....

Picking Up the Pieces

I thought back to right after the funeral when I sat in the living room with Daddy and Mama as they answered countless questions from investigators who were trying to find leads to help them catch her killer. They asked Daddy to make a list of all Kathy's friends and old boyfriends, so they could question each one of them.

I patiently waited for investigators to ask me some questions, too, but they didn't. They never asked me anything. I just sat in a chair beside Daddy and never said a word—just like I had done the many mornings I sat in the backseat of the car on the way to kindergarten. Todd's mom drove his brother, Terry, and me to school, and he would ride along with us in the car each day. I was so shy that I never opened my mouth to say a word the whole way there. I would only smile at them, so they gave me the nickname, "Smiley." I felt like that quiet, shy little girl all over again, but the nickname didn't seem to fit anymore.

The fact that I sat there in silence has always haunted me. I felt guilty thinking I might have been able to tell them something that could have helped find her killer.

Twenty-three years later, on October 1, 2003, just seventeen days before my fortieth birthday, that uncontrollable desire to find out more about what really happened to my sister led me upstairs in Mama's house past Kathy's old room, and into the attic where I knew some of her things were stored. I also knew Daddy and Mama kept all the newspaper clippings of the murder somewhere up there.

As I rummaged through old toys and books, I spotted an area toward the back wall lined with several rows of cardboard boxes. Daddy had meticulously marked each one with her name and the date. I found what I had been looking for.

As I opened each box, a flood of memories poured over me without a dam to hold any of them back. Memorabilia from her short lifetime had turned a slight shade of yellow and collected dust throughout the years. Old and crumbling newspapers found in the boxes gave me insight into the events of that night and the investigation that had begun so long ago. As I sat on the floor in the hot attic reading the details of that night, I relived it. Tears flowed down my cheeks as much then as they did twenty-three years earlier.

One of the articles was written two years after her death, saying that two serial killers, Otis Toole and Henry Lee Lucas, had confessed to killing her. I remembered a few details about the arrest of the men. As a family, we just didn't talk about anything related to her death, so what I knew about the men came from conversations I had with my friends.

Just a few years earlier I had also seen a documentary about the two serial killers and how they had confessed to traveling the countryside killing many women, as well as Kathy. Even though they had confessed to all these crimes, I didn't know if charges had ever been brought against them for her murder because the documentary stated that Lucas and Toole were already serving several life sentences for convictions in other states.

I wasn't sure what I was really looking for that day in the attic, but I knew I had to find answers to some of the questions my daughters were asking; they were the same questions I wanted to ask as a seventeen-year-old high school senior when my world came crashing down.

At the bottom of the last box, I found a small card with a detective's name and phone number written at the top of it. I put the card in the pocket of my jeans and closed up all the boxes. I knew that's where I would begin my search.

I called the number and asked to speak to Ray Vail, the name of the man scribbled on the card, but the officer who answered told me the detective had retired from the sheriff's office several years earlier and was teaching at a local school. It seemed that as fast as the door to the past had opened, it closed just as quickly.

After looking back through all the newspaper clippings I had gathered in the attic, I decided to check with the publisher of the paper to see if there were possibly even more articles about Kathy's murder or about the two serial killers accused of killing her. The publisher said their office didn't have the space to store old newspapers, so they didn't keep any in their building, but he was sure I could find what I was looking for on microfilm at the university library.

A new library had been built since I graduated from the school, and I was thrilled to discover they had a very large collection of early editions of the paper on microfilm. I took off work and spent hours scouring through paper after paper. I made copies of all the related articles and placed them in a folder.

I not only found all the articles I had already read in the attic, I also found articles I had never seen before that were written several months after Kathy's death. A few of them focused on the task force that had been formed by some of the lead detectives to focus on the two serial killers, Lucas and Toole. One article stated detectives from all over the country had met in our area to compare notes in hopes of solving homicides in their own states.

I was physically and mentally exhausted when I left the university that day, but that night, I began scanning each article in my folder for every single detail that might help me understand what happened to Kathy. I underlined parts of the articles I thought were important and started writing notes in a journal to help me keep a record of all the information. I even created a filing system for each article and all of my notes, so I could easily retrieve facts as needed.

I could barely hold my eyes open any longer when I went to bed that evening. As I drifted off to sleep, Lucas and Toole chased me.

I ran.

For the next several years, I had many nightmares like this; and in every dream, her killer had a different face. I dreaded nights because I knew during my sleep I would be forced to stare into the faces of so many monsters.

I just wanted to put a face to her killer and bring that face to justice. So one night as I prayed, I pleaded with God to give me wisdom and open doors that had been closed for over twenty-three years—doors I knew only He could open if this journey was truly His will.

The next morning, I mustered up the nerve to try to contact Mr. Vail again, this time at his school.

"Yes, may I please speak with Ray Vail?"

"Well, he's in class right now. May I take a message?"

I gave the secretary my name and number, and she assured me she would give him a message to call me back when he had a break; I sat by the phone and waited—but not long. Soon after I hung up, he called.

I felt like I had finally made a connection to the past.

"Is this Debbie?"

"Yes, Mr. Vail. Thank you so much for calling me back. I'm sorry to bother you at work, but I'm calling to ask about a murder case that you worked on in 1981. My sister, Kathy, was a college student who was shot and killed near the university. Do you remember working on that case?"

"Yes, I do. I remember it well," he said.

"That's great to hear. If you don't mind, I have some questions that I really hope you can help me answer."

"I'll be glad to answer your questions, but instead of talking over the phone, would you mind meeting me here at my school?" he replied.

"No, I wouldn't mind at all. That would be great. Thank you so much! When would be a good time?"

I was so excited; we agreed on a day and time, and I started jotting down questions that came faster than I could write them down. I knew he would be able to fill in the gaps that had haunted me for so many years, but I was a little nervous about how those gaps might be filled.

⁊

The day Kathy was killed, Daddy and Mama had given us very few details of her death. They told us her car had been hit from behind, and that was probably the reason she stopped in the middle of the road. Her car had been found close to the college where she attended, and her body which had been shot several times was found about a mile away from her abandoned car on a rural roadside. Her little blue Mustang was still running when the police found it, and her purse was left on the front seat of the car. Those were the only facts I knew because my parents wanted to shield us as much as they could from what happened to her.

I really didn't know what other information I expected to gain from my meeting with the detective, but I knew it was at least a starting point.

❧

The night before our meeting, I felt that the months of secrecy needed to come to an end, at least with Todd. As we sat together on the edge of the bed, I opened up my heart to him and revealed everything I had been doing. I was a little worried that he would be upset because he had lived every part of the real-life nightmare with me, and I knew he wouldn't want me to endure any more suffering. Kathy had been like a sister to him, too, so I feared he might not understand my need to open up that hurtful time in my life.

He hugged me tightly and said he understood my need to dig into the past. It was a wonderful feeling to know that someone else knew my secret, and it felt even better knowing that my husband and best friend supported everything I was doing.

I didn't tell anyone other than Todd where I was going that morning because I didn't know if the information I would learn that day would lead me further down my path or stop me dead in my tracks. I knew I had to start somewhere, though, and this investigator's name happened to be the first clue I found. I had no choice but to drive the twenty miles back into my old college town to meet him.

For those twenty minutes, the questions I prepared replayed through my mind. Even with the practice, I was just as nervous as on the first day I returned to high school after Kathy's death. As I drove through the school gate, every part of my body shook. I laughed under my breath because my trembling hands reminded me of Kathy. She always had trouble with nerves. Her hands would shake uncontrollably when she was anxious; even her voice would sometimes tremble when we sang in front of the church.

I decided I wasn't about to let my nerves keep me from getting answers. I took a deep breath to calm myself down and walked into the front office. I stood by the door and waited for the secretary to finish speaking with a student.

"May I help you?" she asked.

"Yes, Ma'am. I have an appointment with Ray Vail. He is expecting me."

"Just have a seat and I'll call him down to the office."

As she turned around to call his name over the intercom, I reached in my purse for a tissue to wipe my hands that had started sweating. It wasn't long before a middle-aged man poked his head around the office door and smiled. He shook my hand and introduced himself as he led me out of the office and into an empty classroom where we would be able to speak privately.

After a few more words of introduction, I thanked him for taking time out of his day to meet with me. I let him know that I had teenage daughters asking questions about their Aunt Kathy—questions I couldn't answer and answers I needed to know myself. He said he understood perfectly why I would want to know the truth, and then he began giving me a very specific timeline of the events that occurred the night of her death.

As he went step-by-step through what happened, I listened intently and wrote down as much as I could. He didn't have any notes in front of him, but was able to give me specific information about the investigation. He might have reviewed his files before meeting me, but I knew he must have been very involved in her case because he recounted all of Kathy's activities on the night of her murder without hesitation.

He explained, "Kathy and the girls she stayed with had gone to one of the college hangouts that Friday night, and then they split up around 1:30 in the morning on Saturday, April 4.

I looked up from notating and nodded as he continued.

A little while later, Kathy went back to the house where she was staying with her friends. When she arrived, she saw they were there with two men she didn't know. Now, at that point, Kathy picked up her purse and let the girls know she was leaving to meet two guys from the university to eat breakfast with them at an all-night diner next to the college."

As I listened, that explanation made sense to me. I'm sure Kathy felt like a fifth wheel, so she left because she had been uncomfortable in that situation.

The detective continued, "Through interviews during the investigation, we were able to confirm that she did eat breakfast that morning at a diner near the university, but she ate alone. Apparently she just made an excuse about meeting the guys, so she could leave the house."

That also made sense to me. I sat on the edge of my seat trying to capture each word.

"Shortly after she left the restaurant, she drove down a road in front of the university where her car was bumped from behind. I'm sorry, but we assumed she got out of her car at that point and that's when the killer abducted her."

Tears started to form, but I fought them back; nothing was going to keep me from remembering every detail.

"When we found her car, the engine was still running, the driver's door was wide open, and we found her purse on the front seat. About an hour after finding the car, an anonymous caller tipped us off that a body had been dumped on the edge of a wooded area down a rural road just a few miles away from the college."

After he had given me the detailed description of Kathy's final moments leading up to her death, he went on to say, "After investigating, we believed Henry Lucas and Otis Toole, two notorious serial killers, were the ones responsible for her death. A task force was formed in February of 1982, and in May of 1983 Lucas became our primary suspect. I personally went to the prisons where they were being held on other charges and interrogated them. Both men gave us quite a few facts that only the killers would have known about the murder; facts that were not released to the public."

"What information are you referring to?" I asked.

"Lucas hit 45-50 points on peak information."

"What do you mean by that?"

"He knew the type of weapon, her car type, and he also knew the car had been bumped. Then in June, we met with Otis Toole, and he hit 95 points."

He went on to tell me that he and the department were convinced Henry Lee Lucas and Otis Toole were her killers.

I was confused. The killers knew a lot of the same information I had read in the old newspapers. I asked myself, *If those facts were made public, then how could they have been details that only her killers would have known?*

I really wasn't prepared for what he said next, though: "Lucas and Toole usually tortured their victims before they killed them."

My stomach tightened again, and I became claustrophobic in our empty room, but I had to know: "Was Kathy tortured?" I held my breath waiting on his response.

"No, they didn't torture her."

My breathing returned to normal, but I was still confused. I quizzed the detective about other murders Lucas and Toole had committed, because in my mind, her murder just didn't fit with the descriptions of the other killings he described. He told me the two men usually stabbed or strangled their victims, and Kathy had been shot.

I thought about the documentary I had seen a few years earlier on Lucas and Toole and how they had confessed to hundreds of murders that were later proven to be false confessions before they both died in prison. Then I asked the question I had wanted to ask for years.

"Was she raped before they murdered her?"

"We couldn't be sure if Kathy was raped. It turns out her ex-boyfriend confessed to us that he had sexual intercourse with her on the day she was killed."

I couldn't wrap my mind around that. It just didn't make any sense to me because I knew she was no longer dating Jessie. Their relationship had already ended many months before she was killed. I also knew how strongly she felt about not having pre-marital sex.

When he finished telling me the events as he remembered them, I teared up as I gave him a hug to let him know how much I appreciated him for meeting with me to help me tie up the loose ends that had been dangling in my mind for so many years.

I left the empty classroom trying to make sense of all the new information. The hallway seemed much longer than when I entered the school. All I wanted to do was get out of that building; my brisk walk turned into a sprint. With each step, overwhelming emotions built up.

When I finally reached my car, my hands were trembling again. I fumbled with my keys, dropped them, picked them up, and fumbled some more as I tried to unlock the door. Sitting in the driver's seat, I burst into a crying fit. I was upset for having to relive Kathy's suffering, and I was angry at myself for waiting so many years to ask these questions. Most of all, I was crying because I didn't think for one minute the men who were accused of killing my sister had actually done it. I knew her real killer was still out there. With that reality firmly set in my mind, I drove home with more questions than answers. Anger trumped sadness, and I became determined to do everything possible to find out who had really killed my sister.

I didn't have any animosity toward this detective who had just helped me force open the pages of my past. I directed my anger only toward myself. *Why had I waited so long to find answers to my questions?* I had no one to blame other than myself.

When I got back to the house, I called Rebecca, one of Kathy's best friends, who had lived across the street from us when we were growing up. I knew she had seen Kathy the day she was killed, and I thought she might be able to confirm or enlighten me about some of my concerns. We talked for quite a while, reminiscing about old times before I explained to her why I was really calling; "I know it's been a long time, and the books are officially closed on the matter, but I'm looking into Kathy's murder, trying to make sense of what happened to her. Can you tell me everything you remember about the day Kathy was killed?"

"Sure, I'll be glad to help. Well, I remember riding home from work with Kathy that day. She dropped me off at my house, and then she left. I didn't see her again. Not much help I suppose."

"It is helpful, and I have to ask one more thing. You were so close to her. Did she ever mention during that ride home about seeing her ex-boyfriend, Jessie, that day?"

"I'm positive she wouldn't have seen him on that day or any other day because they were no longer dating."

I knew how close she had been to Kathy, so I asked one more critical question, "Did Kathy ever confide in you about being sexually active with anyone at all?"

She laughed and assured me, "Kathy was not that kind of girl! But there is one thing that I remember. I saw Kathy's body at the funeral home, and I asked the detectives why her fingernails were cut so short." Kathy had always worn long fingernails. "He told me that they clipped all of her nails in case she might have scratched her killer, so they could check for blood evidence under them."

Of course, there was no such thing as DNA evidence at the time, so searching for blood evidence was pretty common practice. "One more thing," she added, "I also noticed bruises all over her arms and face."

That saddened me all the more, but made me more determined. "I am not going to rest until I find answers to every unanswered question." I was serious about that. The next day, I called the sheriff's department again, and this time I asked to speak to a homicide detective. They put me through to an investigator named Toney. I explained Kathy's case and asked, "Do you remember it?"

"I do ma'am, but I can't really discuss all the details of the investigation because the case is still open."

What? I couldn't believe what I was hearing! *How could the case be open if they had found her killers a few years after her death? What about the confessions of Lucas and Toole?* But I didn't say a word—I just listened.

Toney went on to explain that at his request, the investigation had been reopened; He and Trooper Cummings, a friend with the State Police Department, had been working on the cold case together. Cummings' father was one of the lead investigators who worked on Kathy's case in the 1980's. His father had always regretted not being able to solve it, and that instilled in Cummings a special desire to bring the case to a conclusion.

"I'm confused," I told him. "I met with a former detective, Ray Vail, who worked Kathy's case, too, and he was under the impression that her case had been closed for years because of those confessions by the serial killers."

Toney reassured me that the case was not closed; and in so many words, he informed me that the department no longer believed the two serial killers had murdered her. How relieved I felt to know I wasn't the only one who believed her real killer was still on the loose.

Toney went on to tell me that at the time of Kathy's murder, he was working in the narcotics division, but he remembered how her killing had gripped the entire college community with fear. She was one of three young women who had been murdered in less than a two year time span. Toney never believed Lucas and Toole were guilty of her murder or the other two murders, but there was a lot of pressure from the community at the time to solve her case as well as the two other homicide cases.

All three of the local girls who were killed had been shot within just a few miles of each other. The other two victims were young, white females, and the cases were very similar in nature.

In August of 1980, just eight months before Kathy's murder, a young girl had been killed after she finished her shift and left work for the evening. Her body was found several miles from the convenience store she managed. She had been abducted and taken to another area of town, then shot and killed. When her car was found, the keys were still in the ignition, and the lights were still on.

A few months after Kathy was killed, another girl had been murdered while returning home from visiting her boyfriend, who lived just down the road from her house. Police determined that she was shot through the driver's window of her car. The car was still parked on the highway about a mile from her home when a passing motorist found her body.

Toney believed all three cases were connected, but not the work of Lucas and Toole.

"The only way to prove Lucas and Toole were not the killers," Toney explained, "would be to send DNA evidence, a single hair found on the inside of Kathy's underwear, to the crime lab to rule them out as the ones who raped and killed her."

Raped and killed her?

My heart sank. I swallowed hard as I tried to digest that statement. I could feel my eyes starting to burn from the tears that were welling up inside them. My heart began to beat so fast I thought it would explode. I tried not to show any emotion over the phone, so I just let him continue talking hoping that he wouldn't realize that he had just broken news to me that I had never heard before.

"I'm amazed that DNA evidence from her case is still available, and fortunately, it had been properly stored in our crime lab all these years."

Toney had been investigating two other men for her murder, and he wanted to rule them out using the DNA evidence. Both suspects were career criminals. One man was sitting in a prison in Louisiana about to die, and the other sat in jail across the country in California. He would be collecting DNA from them soon and sending the samples to the lab to be analyzed. He had also requested that the crime scene DNA be compared to Lucas' and Toole's DNA samples that had been taken from them before they died in prison a few years earlier.

When I got off the phone with Toney, I went to my room and broke down in tears. What horror she must have experienced that night!

Why, Lord?

Why would you allow her to experience such terror?

She was so innocent!

Some people tell me it's not possible to hear God answer our prayers, but I know it is possible because on that night, He slipped me another note; this time

II Corinthians 4:18 which reads, "So we do not look at what we can see right now, the troubles all around us, but we look forward to the joys in heaven which we have not yet seen. The troubles will soon be over, but the joys to come will last forever." Even though she suffered, I knew God had been with her that horrible night because she was His child—and the very second she closed her eyes in death—she opened them with Him in the joys of heaven.

Todd also tried to console me as we talked about all the details I got from Toney. I didn't understand how three young, beautiful women in the same community could be killed and their killer never be brought to justice. I couldn't comprehend how a rapist and murderer could still be walking our streets. I knew Toney seemed sure the cases were linked; but in the back of my mind, I still had doubts.

By morning, the drive to get to the truth only grew stronger. I kept thinking about the phone call Kathy got that night from Jessie's girlfriend and what Ray Vail said about how Jessie had confessed to having an intimate relationship with her the day before she was killed. I thought about the words Mamaw spoke the minute she heard of Kathy's death. In my mind I began to think of a different scenario about her death—a scenario that involved Jessie.

He had been taken in for questioning right after her murder, but shortly after his interrogation, the police released him. He came straight to the house, dropped to his knees in almost the exact same spot where Mamaw had fallen to her knees and cried out in anguish as he expressed how much he loved Kathy and that he would have never done anything to harm her. He seemed sincere, but I still wondered if the police had released Kathy's real killer that day.

Months went by after I first talked to Toney; we stayed in contact through phone conversations and emails. I wanted to know everything that was happening as the two men worked together to help catch her killer. Even though I had never seen him in person, I could tell through our phone calls that he was as determined as I was to solve her cold case. I'm sure he sometimes dreaded my phone calls because there were so many; but at that point, I didn't really care. I wanted to know everything.

The Christmas holidays in 2003 came and went, and a new year arrived. I found it harder and harder to keep my work on Kathy's case a secret from my family. I wanted to let them know whoever had committed that evil act was still out there, but Mama was fragile. She had been diagnosed with cancer two years after Kathy's death and had barely survived the treatments. Ten years after her first diagnosis, the cancer came back; but with faith and determination, she had won that battle again. In the meantime, she lost Daddy and both of my grandparents. I couldn't see bringing up the past and making her relive the murder too.

I thought that maybe I could tell Amy and Steve and no one else; but every time I thought about their reaction, I would change my mind:

Are you crazy, Debbie?

Do you want Mama to suffer even more?

Why would you do that to her?

Truthfully, I really didn't know how they would react to the news, but the possibility of opening and deepening old wounds, made me decide to keep it secret. At least I was finally able to tell Toney about the phone call Kathy received on the night she was killed. I made sure he knew about her relationship with Jessie and how they had gone through a pretty rough break up. Kathy didn't see a future with him, but he just didn't want to let her out of his life.

I wasn't sure what would happen with the case; but I continued to pray each night for answers, and I thanked God for helping me release my feelings of guilt through working with Toney. I asked God to lead me further down the path of the past, if that was His will.

I knew Toney and his friend were working diligently to find Kathy's killer, but I found it harder and harder to just sit still and wait for an email or a call to update me with the progress of her case. So I called Toney a lot; he had to be tired of me. It didn't matter. I inherited tons of patience from my daddy but not enough to sustain me through this. The constant doubts didn't help either: *Why am I so involved? Why am I uncovering the pain? Is this God's will or just my own selfishness and vengeance at play?* It seemed that each time I had doubts, answers came, too—this time on the phone:

"What's up, Sis? What have you been up to?"

"Hey Steve. I've just been doing a little housework. Why?"

"Sure you have," he said jokingly.

"Why are you laughing?"

"You've been up to more than that!"

"What are you talking about?"

He laughed again and said, "I just got off the phone with a guy named Toney, and he told me you've been real busy!"

"How did you know?"

"That's the funny part. I didn't. I've just had Kathy's death on my mind for a long time, so I decided to call the sheriff's office to find out more about what really happened to her. They put me through to Toney. After I told him who I was, he

62

chuckled and said, "You haven't talked to your sister, have you?'"

If I ever needed confirmation from God that it was His will for me to be on this journey, I had it! Not only did the police open the investigation again, but God placed the same desire in my little brother's heart and mind around the same time he placed it in my own.

I caught Steve up on everything, and we talked about how we needed to eventually tell Amy. But I was so glad to know Steve wasn't upset, and that he wanted to open up the door to the past and join me in my search for the truth.

One of those doors to the past was Kathy's diary. After the funeral, a detective asked Daddy if she had kept a diary, so he sent me upstairs to her room to get it. I grabbed her journal off her dresser and rushed back downstairs to give it to him. I had forgotten that she also kept a diary under the mattress of her bed. Mama must have found it when she was putting away Kathy's things.

I thought nothing of it until the day I decided to go snooping again. After Mama went shopping with Aunt Jeanette, I hovered over an old trunk at the end of the upstairs hallway. The trunk contained things Mama had packed away from Kathy's room about a year after her death—things she didn't want to have to look at every day. Now, over two decades later, there lay her diary tucked neatly under her blue-and-white-laced bedspread.

I opened the diary with its little key and began reading. Kathy had written entries for almost every day for the two years leading up to her death. I ran downstairs, found a pencil and a piece of paper, and began to jot down a timeline of dates and important events from her writings.

Her stand on premarital sex was right there in black and white in her own handwriting. Through her own words, it was obvious she had not been sexually active with anyone, and she had very strong feelings about that issue. In my eyes that was proof that she did not have consensual sex with Jessie.

I remember when Toney told me over the phone that the DNA evidence and other evidence found at the crime scene suggested she had been raped—it was so hard to take—but I knew it made much more sense than what Ray Vail believed. I knew she would not have willingly been intimate with Jessie or anyone else the day she was killed.

I made copies of the diary for Toney and felt that now, more than ever, I wanted to tell Mama and Amy, but I just couldn't. I didn't want to tell them until I was certain we had found her real killer.

It had been almost an entire year since I started my quest, and I had kept so many secrets; but the secrecy, at least where Amy was concerned, would soon be coming to an abrupt end.

Chapter 6

Unlocked Secrets

Why is he calling?

Amy just stared at his name on the caller ID for a few seconds, a name she hadn't seen in over twenty years. Amy was only a young teenager when Kathy dated Jessie, but she remembered how friendly he was to her and how he used to joke around with her when he came to the house to pick up Kathy.

"Hello?" But she only heard silence, then a dial tone. She immediately called me.

"Guess who just called and hung up?"

"Who?"

"Jessie." As she spoke the name, I went into a state of sheer panic.

"You have to tell me. Have you seen or heard from him at all lately?"

"No, not for years. But I think I saw his company truck a few times on my way to work. What's up? Why do you sound so panicky?"

For the first time since I had opened up the door to the past, I was afraid—afraid he had found out that one of us was trying to reopen her case and that he wasn't happy about it. What other explanation could there be for the call?

"I have to tell you something. Now please let me explain before getting upset at me."

"Okay, what is it?"

"I've been looking into Kathy's murder, and so have the police."

"You've been what? Why?"

"They reopened the case, Amy. They are pretty sure the murderer hasn't been caught."

She wanted to know everything from the very beginning. She quizzed me over and over again about my meeting with Ray Vail and all the phone conversations I had with Toney.

"I understand why you did what you did, but look, I need to be a part of everything from now on. No more secrets."

"Okay. No more secrets."

Steve, Amy, and I agreed that we shouldn't tell Mama yet about what we were doing, especially not after that creepy phone call from Jessie. She would only worry, and we weren't even sure if we would ever get to the truth about what happened to Kathy. There was another thing we all agreed on—we needed to tell Toney about the call.

Even before I could call him, he called me early the next morning.

"Debbie, I've got some news for you."

"I have something I need to tell you too."

"My news isn't so good. The DNA results came back from the lab. I hate to tell you this, but I thought you'd want to know that the two guys I thought did it have been ruled out. We've hit a dead end."

"No, that's not very good news, but I'm so glad you called. Listen, my sister, Amy, got a phone call yesterday. It was so strange because the caller ID showed the name of Kathy's ex-boyfriend, Jessie. But he didn't say anything, just dead silence—then he hung up."

His tone moved from disappointed to concerned, "Let me see how I can collect a DNA sample from him. Maybe we have it on file already, or maybe there's some other way. Does he live close by?"

"Yeah, just in the next town."

As much as I didn't want to believe Jessie killed her, it just seemed like things were pointing in that direction. He and Kathy had double-dated with Todd and me several times before they eventually broke up, and he always seemed like such a nice guy. He definitely didn't seem like a murderer, but I didn't really know him well, and good people can do bad things when they are desperate. From reading her diary, I got the feeling he was pretty desperate to stay in her life.

❦ Chapter 7 ❦

....

Still Out There

My eyes opened from the sunlight coming through my bedroom window, and I immediately thought about Kathy. She had brought such sunlight to our lives for the nineteen years she was with us on this earth, and today was her birthday— September 20, 2005, almost two years after I started my truth journey.

I hadn't heard from Toney in a while so I gave him a call.

"Hey Toney, just checking in to ask if you have anything new to tell me."

I was pretty used to the "No, I don't" replies, so when he said, "Yes, I do," I was pretty excited. "I was actually going to call you today to tell you that Lucas and Toole have also been ruled out—their DNA didn't match." Their faces had haunted me in my nightmares long enough—faces that belonged to men of pure evil. I was so relieved they weren't the ones. How fitting that I got the news on her birthday!

Now I knew beyond a shadow of a doubt that God had a purpose for sending me down this road. The DNA results proved once and for all that her killer was still out there, and he was still capable of bringing the same kind of pain and suffering that my family experienced to another innocent family. He put me in this for a reason.

"There's one more thing I should mention," he said. "Hurricane Katrina has taken Cummings to New Orleans. I'm not sure when I'll work the case again because we're so short-handed right now."

"I understand," I said, but really I was discouraged. I couldn't let things slow down now. More than ever, her killer had to be found.

I spent Kathy's birthday thinking about how we used to celebrate our birthdays when we were little girls. We invited our best friends, Carol and Lori, over for a birthday party. Mamaw fixed cupcakes and put a candle on each one. I knew if I could turn back the clock to one of my own birthdays when we were young kids, I would make a very special wish. I would wish that the events that happened on April 4, 1981, would have never happened. I desperately wished I could celebrate her birthday with her that night, but I was only able to bake a cupcake in her honor and celebrate through my memories.

(picture of Kathy's birthday party)
(From left to right: Amy, Lori, Carol, and me)
(Kathy is in the center.)

🦋 Chapter 8 🦋

....

Secret Meeting

*A*ll I wanted for Christmas in 2005 was for Toney to tell me he had a new lead in the case—or even better—he had solved it. Every time I returned home from shopping for gifts I checked the caller ID to see if I had missed his call. But the holidays rolled by without a word from him.

On January 5, 2006, almost three years after I had started my quest for justice, I called Toney and told him I had been thinking about some of the entries Kathy had made in her diary. I really made the call because it had been so long since we had talked that I just wanted to make sure he hadn't completely forgotten about the case. I think he could hear the desperation in my voice, so he asked, "Would you mind turning over the diary to me so I can take a look at it?"

"No, of course not," I said. I was delighted he had such interest and time. We decided to meet the next day.

I drove into the parking lot at a sandwich shop near the university and just sat and waited. After a few short minutes, a truck turned in from the main road and parked next to the driver's side of my car. The man behind the wheel rolled down his window and smiled at me. It had to be Toney. He stepped out of his truck and walked up to my window. I didn't have a face to put with Kathy's killer, but it was nice to have a face to put with the person who had been helping me find him—the person I believed would eventually catch her killer.

I rolled down the window to greet him.

"Well, I guess you're Debbie."

"And you must be Toney. It's so good to finally meet you in person."

"Debbie, I want you to know I think what you are doing is great. You are such a good sister."

"Toney, I appreciate all that you have done. I really can't thank you enough."

His smile and encouraging words helped me to feel, once again, like I had made the right decision to look into the past. I handed him the diary through the car window.

" I want you to know that we were able to collect a sample of Jessie's DNA. He volunteered to give it to us without any problem. I've already sent it to the crime lab for analysis."

I was so excited!

I thanked him over and over again and reminded him how much my family really longed to have justice for Kathy. I felt like we were on the right track again and the cold case was finally warming up.

❦

When Kathy was killed, I felt like God had to pick me up each morning and help me make it through the day. At this point in my life, almost twenty-five years later, I was having those same needs. I prayed every night that God would pick me up again, just like he had done then, and help me do the things a mother of two young teenagers had to do. I prayed He would keep me strong and help me find answers for my family.

After the girls went to bed at night, I would often take out all of my folders and sit in the middle of the bedroom floor and comb through all of the information I had collected. I read each news article over and over looking for a clue that I might have missed.

I read the entries from Kathy's diary many times, too—just so I could feel close to her, and remember her.

In February, I made another call to Toney; Trooper Cummings was still in New Orleans, and there was no new information to tell me. The DNA lab was so backed up that the results of Jessie's DNA report had not been returned yet. Months and months went by. I sent emails and made regular calls to Tony, but each time he regrettably had no new leads. With every passing day, I found myself falling further and further into a deep valley of despair.

∽

The day after Kathy was killed, I locked myself in my room and cried out to God pleading with him to turn back the hands of time to the time she left the house. I wanted to have a chance to make her change her mind so she would stay home with me that night. I would have done anything to keep her from facing the brutal death she faced.

Through my tears, God revealed to me that once Jesus also pleaded with His Father to take away the terrible death He would have to face on an old rugged cross—if there had been any other way for man to be saved—He asked His Father to make it so. As I sat there crying, God reassured me that just as His plan of salvation through the sacrifice of His Son was part of His perfect plan, what happened to Kathy was part of a plan I couldn't comprehend; but nevertheless, a perfect plan.

❧ *Chapter 9* ❧

....

Help Sent from Heaven

Twenty-five years to the day that Kathy was killed (on April 4, 2006), Toney called.

"Jessie's DNA results are in."

"Yes, and...?"

"They're not a match."

"I don't understand. What about the mysterious call to Amy? What about the fact that Ray Vail had led me to believe that Jessie had been with Kathy on the day of her murder? What about the phone call his girlfriend made to her the night before she was killed?" Poor Toney. I threw all my frustration at him. I knew we had come to an impasse. No leads—no DNA match—nothing. I needed my mama.

On that anniversary night, I sat Mama down and told her all the details of my journey. She wasn't mad at me for opening old wounds—not at all, but she was disappointed I hadn't shared everything with her. As we relived the past, we didn't feel very confident her killer would be found in the near future. We both felt so helpless that night.

When Mama left, I prayed that God would show me which way to turn, which way to go to start a new path that would lead to justice for Kathy. I sat down, and through my tears wrote a poem.

Oh God, I cry up to the heavens;
Do you hear my voice?
The pain is so great to bear;
Do you hear my voice?
My tears are tears of sorrow;
Do you hear my voice?

Lift me up Lord;
Please hear my cry.
Send your love and help me hear you;
I need to hear your voice.
I hear your voice when I see your wonders;

I can hear your voice.
When I think of what you did for me;
I can hear your voice.
Your words are my only comfort;
Through them, I hear your voice.

Help me, Lord, to open my ears.
Help me hear your voice.
I need your voice to calm my fears.
I need your voice to bring me cheer.
Oh Lord, I'll listen please speak to me.
I need thee Lord, this is my plea;
Oh speak to me, Oh speak to me.

Halfway through writing my psalm of despair, I felt an overwhelming calmness throughout my entire body. Through the writing of my heart, God reminded me He was still in charge, and He still had a voice in everything that was happening. Most importantly, He was hearing my voice! I went to bed that night with the reassurance that God had heard my voice, and He would answer my prayers in His own way—in His own time—not mine.

The next day I had a new sense of calmness; but at the same time, I had a new sense of urgency that I knew could only come from God. I got on the Internet and randomly searched. I didn't know exactly what I was searching for, but I just couldn't sit still and do nothing. I looked up other unsolved murders and somehow came across a group called the Vidocq Society.

What caught my attention was the society's credo, "Veritas Veritatum – The Truth of Truths." My heart longed for the truth about what happened to Kathy. I kept reading.

Their website said that the society is an exclusive crime-solving organization that meets monthly in Philadelphia, Pennsylvania. It was formed in 1990 and named after the famous 18th century French detective, Eugene Francois Vidocq. The members apply their collective skills to solve cold case homicides and unsolved deaths. The society is composed of over eighty-four men and women from around the world with various backgrounds, such as detectives, former FBI agents, and forensic scientists.

After reading their mission of helping to solve long-standing, unsolved murders, I knew I had to write a letter asking them to consider taking Kathy's case. It would be a long shot, but I didn't have anything to lose, and I had nowhere else to turn.

On their website, it also stated the society had very strict guidelines. If they took a case, they would never contact or speak to members of the victim's family about how they were working to solve it or the progress they were making. They would only talk to the local law enforcement officers, and they would only investigate unsolved homicides when the local law enforcement agencies accepted their support. I could handle any guidelines they threw at me as long as they would take her case.

I didn't know how Toney and the sheriff's office would feel about allowing people outside their department to hear the details of a case they hadn't yet solved, but I just seemed to be pushed in the society's direction and had to wonder, with all the other providences, if finding them was another guiding hand from God. I sat down at my computer and composed a letter. I included all the details I knew about Kathy's case. I wanted them to have a face to put with the victim, so I copied the family portrait we had made shortly before Kathy's death and put it in the letter. I mailed it the next day on April 16, 2006.

Months went by without a reply. Then, on July 16, 2006, I decided I had waited long enough. I sent an email asking if I would be notified as to whether or not they had taken her case.

That night before I went to bed, I checked my email. I could hardly contain the excitement seeing their name in my inbox. They said they had been in communication with the sheriff's department about her case, and they were waiting for the sheriff to make a decision as to whether or not he would accept the society's help. The email confirmed that they would not be able to help me unless they had full cooperation from the agency that was handling the investigation. I yelled from the kitchen for Todd to come and read the email; I called Amy, Steve, and Mama, too, to share the good news.

It was a new year, and it seemed like it might just be the year we would find justice for Kathy. Even though I questioned God almost daily about whether or not I was doing the right thing, He reminded me through this small miracle that He was at work because the Vidocq Society only accepted one or two cases from all over the world each year, and they wanted to take her case.

❧ Chapter 10 ❧

....

Waiting

A few weeks before my birthday, I finally heard from Toney. He called to let me know that the Vidocq Society had contacted them, and the department had agreed to accept their help. Ironically, he would be traveling to Philadelphia on my birthday, October 18, 2006, to present Kathy's case to the society.

I could not have received a better birthday present; now there would be a whole group of professionals working to solve her murder, and her case would be back in the forefront of the department.

When October 19th came, I was a nervous wreck just thinking about Toney presenting Kathy's case that day. I closed my eyes and imagined all the experts working together in their large meeting hall, combing through the old evidence and strategizing their next move.

I had spent a lot of time on their website reading about the members of the society, and their credentials were impeccable. I had more hope than ever that we were close to catching her killer. I prayed and thanked God for the new direction He was leading me in my search for answers.

A few days later, on October 22, Toney contacted me. He shared how he had presented the details of Kathy's murder to the group and answered their many questions. He explained that several members of the society were interested in his presentation and had requested additional information from him. Another investigator, Medaries, who had worked on Kathy's case for many years, also went with Toney; he had spent several hours after the meeting with a few members of the society who wanted to hear even more. One member requested a copy of Kathy's autopsy report. Their interest encouraged me.

I'm sure Toney didn't tell me everything that transpired during the meeting, but from what he did tell me, I knew several people were looking at the facts from various perspectives and specialties.

Months passed and another holiday season came and went with the usual emails and calls to Toney with no new updates. After each passing day, I felt the case getting colder and colder again.

On January 13, 2007, I emailed Toney just to let him know I would never give up even though in my heart I felt like the case was losing steam.

Toney,

Hope that you had a good holiday! I've been very anxious to touch base with you about any new developments with the case. I tried not to bother you during the holidays, but I am very curious to see if there have been any new developments. Here are a few questions I've had on my mind:

1. *Have any of the Vidocq members been in contact with you since your meeting in Philadelphia?*
2. *Were you able to send the autopsy report to them?*
3. *Is there any way to get Kathy's case picked up by the media?*

Every day my mind races with thoughts about the events of that night and the weeks after her death. I miss her so much, and I just want you to know I will never give up! My family and I want to thank you for what you are doing for us. Please know that we appreciate your dedication to solving her murder.

Thank you so much!
Debbie

I didn't understand why God would take us this far without a resolution. The pieces of the puzzle were just not fitting together like I had envisioned. The Vidocq Society was supposed to be on the case; and after twenty-five years, it seemed like her killer should have been brought to justice by now. I didn't understand why God wasn't allowing a faster resolution.

∾

When my youngest daughter, Katelyn, was little she loved putting puzzles together. Sometimes I would go in the room where she was working and try to put some of the pieces in place. I would always look at the box, so I could see what the final picture should look like.

At that point in my life, I was frustrated because living from day to day was like trying to work a giant puzzle with no clear picture of what the end result would look like. Waiting on the Lord to reveal His will and His purpose meant I would never have the whole picture in front of me to show me His entire plan. I knew I had to live each moment like I was placing a single piece at a time in the giant puzzle of life. As hard as it was to face that fact, I could take comfort in knowing that He knew exactly what the final picture would look like. After all, He is God.

❧ *Chapter 11* ❧

....

We Got Him!

" *H*ey sis, you sitting down?"

"Yeah, why?"

"Toney just called and said they have a hit—a match for the DNA."

"Are you serious?"

"Yeah, he sent it to some FBI database and they found a match."

On March 27, 2007, over three years after I started my truth quest, we got a hit. Toney sent the old DNA sample to CODIS, the FBI's Combined DNA Index

System Program that contains DNA samples taken from criminals nationwide and a match was found.

After I hung up the phone, I frantically searched my wallet for Toney's number. I needed to hear the news straight from him.

"Steve told me you got a match on the DNA." I was almost yelling into the phone from my excitement. "Who is it? Who did it?"

"Now, Debbie, this isn't like the television shows where stuff happens instantly. It's going to take a little time."

Toney explained that it would take a week or so to get the letter from CODIS giving details about the match. The lab had only spoken to the department over the phone about the hit, but they would be receiving an official letter from them within days. Then the department would have to find the person that CODIS had identified and then get another swab containing DNA and send it to the lab to confirm the match.

I knew after hearing the good news, we would finally have a face to put with her killer. Our whole family met at Mama's house that night and talked for hours. Justice for Kathy was finally within our grasp!

I couldn't sleep at all that night, so I got out of bed in the middle of the morning hours and wrote an email to Toney:

Toney,

I'm so excited that I can't sleep! How can I possibly sleep when I know we are so close to catching her killer! There have been so many times that I thought we were never going to find justice for Kathy. Sometimes I wondered if the person who murdered her was even still alive after so many years. Well, now we know he is alive—and he's out there—somewhere. We have to find him and bring him to justice! Your work is almost over.

Thank you!

Debbie

On March 31, 2007, only days before the twenty-sixth anniversary of Kathy's death, Toney called my cell phone. I had talked to him many times on the phone before, but this time I heard a tone of excitement I had never heard in the past. He told me I probably needed to sit down before he gave me the news.

There I was in the middle of a crowded department store in the mall on what would be one of the most important days of my life, trying to find a private place to listen to what he had to tell me. I sat in the middle of a table of neatly folded shirts in the back of the store and tried to press the phone tightly to my ear so I wouldn't miss a single word.

They had a name for the person who had killed my sister; and when they put his name in their computer system, they discovered he had an outstanding warrant for a parole violation. The man was a career criminal who had been arrested more than forty times. Some of those arrests were for violent offenses and he had at least one conviction on his record for sexual assault.

I covered my mouth when I found out the man they were looking for was still living only a few miles from where Kathy had been murdered. At that very moment, the local police and the Louisiana State Police were searching for him.

Warm tears of heartfelt thanksgiving fell down my cheeks as I held up my hands in the air to give God praise for what Toney had just told me. I didn't care who was around me or what they thought about me. Nothing mattered to me except giving praise to God who had heard my prayers.

The scene reminded me of the story in the Bible when Hannah, who was worshipping in the temple, cried out to the Lord for a child because she was barren. The priest thought she was drunk. Her tears were tears of anguish and despair. I knew what it felt like to cry those kinds of tears because I had cried them so many times before.

My anguish had disappeared and relief and joy filled its place. I practically ran out of the mall, got in my car, and called Todd to tell him the good news. Driving home all I could think about was how faithful God had been during my journey. He started it in my heart and He is ending it in the courthouse: "Thank you Jesus! Thank you Lord! God, you are so good!" I said, all the way home.

Doubt always seems to ride on the tail of faith. When I arrived back at the house, I began pacing the floor, wondering, *Could this really be happening? Could this be our day of justice?*

I kept checking the phone to make sure it was on the hook in case Toney tried to call. Then it happened. The phone rang. I raced to the counter and picked up the receiver. Toney said three of the most beautiful words I've ever heard.

"We got him!"

Someone had turned him in for a reward of $500.00. This time instead of an anonymous tip leading police to my sister's body, the anonymous tip led them to a small bedroom in a house where her killer was found hiding under a blanket, smoking a cigarette.

∽

God revealed His power that day in such a mighty way. The man who made the arrest and placed the handcuffs on her killer was the same rookie cop who had been the first policeman on the scene twenty-six years earlier when Kathy's body was found.

Toney gave me the name of the man they had in custody, and I knew what I had to do. When I hung up the phone, I went straight to my computer to find his picture; he would be registered on the state police website since he had a criminal record for sexual abuse offenses in the past.

Within minutes, his face popped up on my screen. I just sat there frozen—for the longest time—just staring at him.

I finally had a face to put with the person who took my sister away from me in such a cruel and brutal way. Surprisingly, as I stared into his eyes, I didn't have feelings of anger, only relief. I felt relief because he would no longer have the freedom to hurt anyone else like he had hurt my sister and my family. His freedom had ended just as abruptly as he had ended Kathy's life, and my journey finally ended, too, so I thought.

Chapter 12

Unexpected Encounter

On Easter Sunday that year, my family had two reasons to celebrate during our church service. We thanked God for Jesus's death and resurrection, and we also thanked Him for allowing us to find the man we believed had killed Kathy. We decided to do something very special that morning.

Kathy always wrote in journals and wrote poetry to express her feelings. During her high school years, she became a member of the journalism club and wrote several poems for the school paper. Most of her poetry centered around her relationship with Christ. She wasn't shy at all about letting people know where she stood concerning her faith. We put one of her poems in a frame and displayed it in the church to honor her memory and her love for what God had done for her when He resurrected that Easter morning thousands of years earlier.

Easter

Yellow, orange, blue, and green
A rainbow of colors announcing spring
A world full of beauty on Easter morn
Reminding the world that all life is reborn
A chance to forget the old and start again
Filling in a part of God's salvation plan
It is the time to renew our faith and trust
And a time to remember what He has done for us

I read her poem one last time that morning before placing the frame back on the table. It seemed like the words were speaking directly to me: *A time to forget the old and start again.* I could hear her saying in her sweet voice, *Debbie, it's time for you to forget those painful memories and start remembering me in a new way. Remember that I'm with the Father and remember what He did for us on that resurrection day. He gave me everlasting life!*

❦

The next day, Toney called.

"We're charging Kathy's killer for murder tomorrow. The department would like your family to be there when we announce it to the public."

"That's wonderful news, Toney! It's truly a blessing!"

"Can you meet me at the court house? When you get there, I'll show you where to go for the news conference."

I was so ready to get there, but it seemed like that twenty-minute ride took forever. My stomach was full of butterflies, this time. No more knots. We would finally be starting the justice process for Kathy. The only regret I had about that day was that Daddy—who died of cancer in January of 2002—couldn't be there to share in the joy and excitement of that moment. I'll never forget the words he said during his final days with us.

"Well, I don't know whether I will be spending Christmas with y'all or with Kathy this year." He spent Christmas with us, but shortly after New Year's Day, he went on to be with the Lord and was reunited with his daughter in the joys of heaven.

As we drove up in the parking lot on that beautiful, sunny day, I was more excited than I had ever been in my life. Mama, Steve and his wife Kim, Amy and her husband Sonny, and Todd and I walked quickly across the busy parking lot. I grabbed the handle of the glass door to the old court house building and pulled it open, not realizing how close I was about to get to my past.

As we entered the main hallway, the sheriff deputies were leading a man in an orange jump suit, arms decorated with tattoos, and shackles on his hands and feet down the stairs toward us. I recognized him immediately from the picture on the sex offender website. He came closer to us and we came closer to him until we all stood face-to-face with the man who stole my sister's life.

Even though I knew he had evil in his heart, when I looked into his face, I felt no bitterness or hatred toward him at all. I also didn't feel scared or threatened like I'm sure my sister did the night he confronted her. I felt powerful and strong. He no longer had any control over my life. When I stared at him, I didn't see a monster—I just saw a man—a man who had done a very evil thing.

Toney took us to a room upstairs where we were to wait.

"I'm sorry about that, really," Toney said. "I had no idea they would be booking him right now."

He didn't know, but God knew. Maybe God allowed me to come face-to-face with her killer in order for me to come face-to-face with twenty-six years of a past I hadn't talked about or let go of. Maybe seeing him in real life, just a few feet away from me, would allow me to finally close the door to the past for good.

It seemed like we waited in the little holding room forever. When Toney finally came to get us, he had more news.

"We're still going to have the press conference, but there won't be any charges filed yet. The district attorney wants a solid case before they charge him, and there's missing evidence. It's not going to happen today."

I can't say we weren't disappointed and fearful that he would get away with the murder like so many of his other crimes. He had been arrested many times in the past, but had never done any significant jail time. He had even been arrested in California a few years before Kathy's murder for a sexual assault against a fourteen-year-old girl. If he had done his original jail time, he would have been in prison in California on April 4, 1981, instead of on McGuire Ranch Road, where he raped and killed my sister.

Toney took us to a crowded room where the press conference had already started. All of us squeezed in and stood against the wall beside Toney, listening to the sheriff give a statement to newspaper reporters and several television camera crews. He explained the details of the DNA match and assured everyone that he expected charges would be filed soon, not only in Kathy's homicide case but possibly two other cold cases.

As the sheriff was finishing his statement, he pointed to Toney and congratulated him on a job well done. Toney smiled, but he was very quick to say, "It's because of the love of a sister that this case is almost closed," and he looked over and pointed at me.

All of a sudden, every television camera pointed straight at me. Just as time seemed to stand still when Daddy said, "Kathy's gone," time also seemed to stop as the cameras turned and faced me.

In that brief silence, I remembered the poem I had written that night when I was in such a deep valley of depression, thinking we had hit a dead end. I desperately asked God if He heard my voice—my voice that was crying out for answers.

In the midst of the bright lights and questions, I wasn't that scared seventeen-year-old teenager sitting in the den with my parents and the detectives, keeping my mouth closed, just listening. I was a grown woman who finally had a voice. God had heard my voice and now he was allowing others to hear my voice too. So I spoke:

"I want everyone here to know how grateful my family is to Toney, and to all the people in the department who didn't let her case die. It's wonderful to finally begin the justice process for Kathy. I also want to thank the Vidocq Society who flew detectives to Philadelphia to help look for answers. We don't really know to what extent they had in helping to catch her killer, but I want to thank them for using their valuable time and resources to help bring justice for my sister."

Steve went on to say, "Our family wants you to know that we have already forgiven the man who is in custody—but justice has to be served—he has to pay the price for what he did to Kathy."

When the press conference was ending, we passed out a statement we had written together, as a family, that explained how much we appreciated each member of the department for all of the countless hours they had spent working on Kathy's case.

In the statement we also mentioned how Kathy had written an autobiography a few months before her death, in which she had written about her faith in God and her future here on earth.

We explained that the man in custody might have taken away Kathy's future on earth, but he could never take away what she cherished most, the eternal life she had received because of her faith in Jesus Christ. We asked the community to pray for our family as we would begin the long process of getting justice for Kathy, and we also asked them to pray for the man who had killed her as well.

That afternoon when we returned home from the press conference, a news reporter from our local paper called and asked if he could take a picture of us around Kathy's gravestone to go along with a story he was writing. He wanted to focus on how our family had lived by faith through all the years after Kathy's death and how as a family, we had finally come to the place where we could say we had forgiven her murderer.

Mama, Steve, Amy, and I stood by her graveside on a beautiful, sunny day—a perfect picture-taking day. I read again, the tribute, etched on the long, gray slab underneath Kathy's tombstone, written by the youth at Greenacres Baptist Church and read by her best friends at her funeral:

Today, Kathy, our dear sister and friend, we want to thank you for the many ways that you've bright-ened each of our lives. We'll always be grateful to you for your willingness to listen to us when we needed a listening ear. Your smiling eyes and thoughtful ways will be etched in our hearts and minds forever. Your love for life was always evident in the little things you did. You expressed your love for us in many different kinds of ways and you always loved us in spite of our faults or shortcomings. With you, we could truly be ourselves and in doing so, we experienced a common bond with one another. Thank you, Kathy, for making us laugh when we didn't always feel like it and for lifting our spirits when they were down. Now we pray for strength to possess the kind of strength and zest that you, yourself, had for life, and we know that God wanted that zest in heaven. Yes, and now there is one more alto voice in that heavenly choir.

I left the cemetery reassured not only of our judicial victory, but also that Kathy led a life of victory here on earth, and she continues to do so in heaven.

The article appeared on the front page the next day. Before I read the story though, I glanced at the picture. There in the distance behind all of us stood a utility pole that looked just like a cross. How fitting to be reminded that the forgiveness we felt for her killer was only made possible because of what happened on the cross; Jesus died and was resurrected so we would also be forgiven and could have eternal life if we believed in His sacrifice.

Left to right – Debbie, Mama, Steve, and Amy

The press conference played on all the local news channels that night. After the broadcast, I got calls from so many of Kathy's old friends thanking my family for not giving up on finding her killer.

We did a lot of celebrating that night. We didn't just celebrate the fact that we had brought her killer to justice. We celebrated Kathy's life by reminiscing about all the good memories we had of her life. We fondly remembered the many nights Kathy, Amy, Steve, and I spent singing gospel songs in harmony with Daddy's wonderful bass voice while Mama played the piano. We reminisced about holidays and vacations we had spent together. We knew from that point forward, her name would be mentioned many more times in our family conversations, and we would no longer avoid talking about our memories of her. The dark cloud which had hovered over our family for decades had finally been lifted, and the silence finally broken.

On April 4, 2007, twenty-six years to the day of her death, Steve made a call to Jessie. He knew he needed to call him because for a time, we believed he was responsible for Kathy's death, and our family needed to ask him to forgive us for suspecting him for so many years. Steve also wanted to make sure he knew that her real killer had been found.

When Steve made the call, he wasn't home, but his wife gave Steve his cell phone number so he could call him at work. When she called out the numbers, a big smile came across his face—his phone number was only one digit away from Amy's home telephone number—another mystery solved.

Steve had a long talk with Jessie, and he was so glad my brother took the time to call. He expressed how much he had enjoyed the time he was able to spend with our family when he was dating Kathy. He felt such relief when he found out that her killer had been arrested—and she would finally receive the justice she deserved.

∽

To this day we still have some unanswered questions though. Did he really make a confession about being with her that night or did Ray Vail get his facts wrong? I'm confident God will reveal the truth about that, too, because God is the revealer of all truth, in His time.

Chapter 13

Was It Worth It?

Less than twenty-four hours after the press conference, Toney called. I just assumed he was calling to congratulate us again or tell us about another newspaper interview that someone wanted us to do.

"Debbie, I hate to have to tell you this, but I've got some pretty bad news."

What could possibly be so bad? I thought, only half believing him.

"We can't find Kathy's autopsy report and pictures from the crime scene are also missing. Without any solid proof it would be very difficult to bring charges against him."

"What are you saying? What does that mean?"

"It means the district attorney has decided not to bring charges against him at this time because of the lack of evidence."

I stood stunned and still.

"The department did an exhaustive search, but the autopsy report is just not here. The coroner may have never written up an official report."

Toney said he didn't know the autopsy report was missing until the Vidocq Society requested a copy. That's when he began searching for it. Without the autopsy report it would be hard to prove Kathy had been raped, so the DNA left at the scene would be useless. Trooper Cummings and other officers in the department had searched frantically for it; but after an exhaustive search, they had not been able to locate it.

I questioned him further and said I understood, but I really didn't understand at all. I hung up and just sat there in my kitchen staring into space in utter disbelief. How could evidence just go missing? I was livid! We had just planted our victory flag on the mountaintop, and now we were wandering aimlessly in the deepest valley we could have ever imagined.

Human nature kicked in, and I started the blame game. My first victim was the district attorney. His job was to take the bad guys off the street and lock them away. Didn't he understand that the man sitting in jail on a warrant violation was a killer? Could he not see that the man behind bars had taken away something irreplaceable to my family?

After I let off some steam and shed a lot of tears, I came to a reasonable calm. The district attorney wasn't to blame—He didn't have a case! He had nothing to back up the CODIS hit.

How could he go to trial with no physical evidence to back up his accusations? If he had taken the case to trial, it would have been thrown out; or even worse, he might take him to court without enough evidence, and he would be found innocent. Maybe I'm to blame. Did God really place the desire in my heart to reopen her case, or did I strike out on my own, seeking justice without His approval?

These thoughts kept beating me up, and more kept coming:

What have I done to my family? I've opened up a Pandora's Box, and now we're going to have to watch as this man walks the streets again knowing what he did to an innocent girl. He might even do the same thing again to someone else.

God gave me a voice to speak to Him, and I knew He heard me before, so I spoke earnestly to Him again.

Please, God, help me understand how, after so many years, we could be so close to bringing her killer to justice only to watch justice slip through our fingers.

At that moment, I couldn't cry out to God any more. I had no more words to say. I had no more tears. I just fell to the floor on my knees in silence. That's when I experienced what I heard my pastors talk about in church while growing up. The words written in Romans 8:26 became real to me for the first time:

"The Holy Spirit prays for us with groanings that cannot be expressed in words."

The Holy Spirit had to pray for me because my mind went numb, and I could no longer pray for myself. My heart was so heavy that it felt like it would bust! In the quiet stillness of that moment, God picked me up out of my anguish and grief and gave me an indescribable peace about the entire situation that flowed through my whole being. It was a peace that could only come from Him.

I had read about that type of peace many times in my daily Bible readings, but I had never experienced it—not to that degree. God reminded me that His plan was perfect and mine wasn't. He was God—and I wasn't!

God assured me that His plan was still in play, even if it wasn't my plan. But everyone at work and all of our friends just assumed that charges had already been brought against Kathy's killer because that's what all the news broadcasts reported—so I had to keep a smile on my face every time someone congratulated me for helping catch him. I had a silent peace, but I also had a secret I couldn't bear to tell them. In my heart I knew that he wasn't charged, and he might never be brought to justice—especially when we heard that the retired coroner who performed the autopsy had no recollection of the case at all—and he didn't have any notes in his files about the murder.

How could a coroner in such a small city not remember a case that rocked a community and crushed a family's world? Every news outlet had blasted details of the case for months after Kathy's death.

We couldn't fathom the incompetence!

My family decided to do everything we could to help find the missing report. I found a copy of Kathy's death certificate in the attic, but not the autopsy report. We contacted the funeral home in hopes they might have kept a copy in their records, but that only led to another dead end.

I even contacted a Texas Ranger I read about in one of the old newspaper articles I found in the attic. He was one of the commanders in 1983, when the task force met about the confessions of Lucas and Toole, so I thought he might have kept copies of some of the old case files. When I called, he was out of town, but his son searched through all of his father's old files and found nothing.

Amy called our local police department thinking they might have filed a copy of it since some of their officers were on the task force formed to interrogate Lucas and Toole. They didn't save any of the old records either.

As another long shot, I called Kathy's doctor hoping they might possibly have a copy, but their search turned up nothing as well.

It seemed that all of our leads kept leaving us empty-handed.

Mama remembered the last name of another detective that worked on Kathy's case, who no longer worked for the sheriff's office. I called every person in the phone book with the last name of Reighney until I finally reached the detective's cousin who graciously gave me his number.

Hope stirred a little when the detective said he definitely remembered her case, so I told him the whole story about finding a DNA match to the crime scene evidence.

"Excellent work!" he said. "I never believed Lucas and Toole were the ones that killed your sister."

"Thank you, but we have a problem. I need to ask if you remember viewing the autopsy report."

"Sorry. I never saw the report, but I know an autopsy was performed because I was standing right there when it happened. I asked for the report a few days later, but the coroner's office never produced it. The sheriff at the time had even written a letter to the coroner requesting the report, but I never saw it, and I don't think it was ever sent."

"—and the crime scene photos and negatives are missing too," I said.

"That's really odd. I know the commander in charge at that time, and he ran a tight ship. I can't imagine that happening under his watch."

After hanging up the phone, I emailed Toney because I had to vent. I didn't understand how so much evidence could just disappear. How could someone walk into an evidence room and take out all the crime scene photos and other pieces of evidence linked to Kathy's case without being noticed? I didn't understand, and I grew very frustrated.

❧

I believe with all my heart that God always hears our prayers and answers them according to His will. Sometimes our prayers are answered right away like we want; other times, they will be answered in God's timing and not our own. We were spiraling down in a sea of despair thinking God had been silent during this time; but in reality, He really was answering our prayers—we just didn't realize it.

Across town in an office in the court house, sat a man named Stephen Sylvester, an assistant district attorney. His life had been consumed for quite some time with cases of rapes, murders, and other violent crimes he had prosecuted. He poured out his heart and soul into his work on a daily basis and became weary from the daily exposure to such horrific images.

One night after returning home from the office after another gruesome day of viewing body parts and reading intimate details not even fit for the big screen, he got down on his knees and asked God for help.

"Lord, I need a break. Please, God, give me a break. I need a simple case—a simple burglary case would be fine."

A few days later, the district attorney, Jerry Jones, walked into his office and handed him a folder.

"I've got a new case I need you to work on."

"What's it about?"

"It's a burglary," said Mr. Jones.

Mr. Sylvester took the folder from his hand with relief and prayed a silent thank you to God for answering his prayer.

No more rapes or murders for a while, he thought.

He sat down and started flipping through the folder; a huge smile came across his face. *God, you sure do have a sense of humor!*

The case before him was a burglary case, but the man accused of the crime was the man believed to be Kathy's killer. Sure, it was just a burglary, but it would be one of the most important burglary cases he would ever try. I believe he worked harder than he had ever worked to make sure he was well prepared for the simple—yet not so simple—case.

Lord, don't let me mess this one up! he thought, knowing that if he botched up this particular case, a suspected killer would be walking the streets again. It also weighed heavily on his mind that the outcome of the case would have a huge impact on one family's life—mine.

....

Chapter 14

The Trial

There was an air of anticipation in the court room as the trial began on July 16, 2007. The news media crowded into the court house, and the court reporter began recording as the first motion was made. The defendant's lawyer, Mr. Thomas, stood before the court and said, "I'm going to make a motion for a change of venue and offer a newspaper article into evidence. The defense believes this article may have tainted the jury pool."

The defense was referring to an article in the local paper that appeared that morning. The headline read,

"26-Year-Old Murder Case Has a Suspect in Custody," which included a picture of the defendant and contained all the information about how he was linked to DNA evidence in Kathy's murder.

The judge stated that he saw the article on the newspaper website that morning and told the court he would put the news article in the record. He explained that he would make inquiry to the jury by calling the panel of potential jurors in and asking them for a show of hands to see if any of them had seen the article that morning or heard information pertaining to Kathy's case on the news.

After he asked jurors about the news article, several people raised their hands to show they had seen it. He said, "In order for the state to get a fair trial and in order for the defendant to get a fair trial, we need a jury, we need individuals who will come and sit in that jury box with no preconceived notions about the case, no opinions about the facts that are involved in the case that have been formed ahead of time." The judge went on to give the jury their instructions and told those potential jurors that if they could not be impartial because of the information they had heard, they would need to let the lawyers know during questioning. He explained that the man on trial was charged with simple burglary.

The assistant district attorney, Mr. Sylvester, questioned members of the jury pool first. He asked them what they considered to be the definition of a burglary. He said, "The first thing I have to prove is that the defendant made an unauthorized entry into a vehicle with the intent to commit a theft. And what is a theft?—the taking of anything of value with the intent to permanently deprive the other person of it."

He asked one of the juror members, "If I prove to you that the defendant went into somebody's vehicle—he didn't have permission to get inside that vehicle—and once inside that vehicle, he took one penny and put it in his pocket, have I proved burglary?"

"Yes,"the juror said.

"But he only took a penny."

"Well, then it's a very small burglary," said the juror.

"Okay, while he was in the vehicle taking the penny, let's say that the owner of the vehicle came out and caught him before he got out of the vehicle. Have I proved a burglary?"

"I think so."

"Okay. And why is that?" asked Mr. Sylvester.

"Well, I would say he intended to take the penny or he wouldn't have put it in his pocket."

"Exactly. And he went into the vehicle that he wasn't authorized to go into, and he took the penny. Right?"

"Right," said the juror.

Then Mr. Sylvester pulled a coin from his pocket and asked a different juror to take a look at it. "It says, 'you are my brother. You are my friend. My bond with you will never end.' I've got two brothers and all three of us have this same coin. Do you think that coin means anything to me?"

"Yes, I do."

"Do you think it has value to me?"

"Yes, it does," said the juror.

"But you can't spend that at the store, can you?"

"No you can't."

"But if somebody went into my vehicle and took that coin and put it in their pocket, do you think that would prove elements of a burglary?"

"Yes."

Mr. Sylvester questioned all the potential juror members, asking them to give him a definition of theft. Most of their definitions were the same; someone taking something that didn't belong to them with no intention of returning the stolen property.

❦

If the jurors only knew what my family believed to be true. The defendant was guilty of much more than simple burglary. The burglary he committed against my family took Kathy away from us; a beautiful human being worth more than money could buy. He had no intention of returning her to us after he took her from her car that night. He knew when he shot and killed her that she would never return to us. In my eyes he was guilty!

∾

After several hours of questioning, by both Mr. Sylvester and Mr. Thomas, the judge asked the potential jurors to leave the courtroom. He asked one potential juror to stay behind—a man who had raised his hand when asked if he had read the newspaper article about Kathy's cold case being solved.

"I wanted to ask you about that newspaper coverage. What do you remember about the article?"

The juror said, "It said they arrested the defendant in someone's car."

"Do you recall anything else about the article? Anything that sticks out in your mind?"

"Well, I mean, they were trying to tie him to some other crimes," answered the juror.

"Do you recall what other crime it was?

"It was a murder case, I believe."

Mr. Thomas asked, "What about the fact that the paper tried to tie him to some other case?"

"Well, that's an old trick to try too. You solve a bunch of them all at one time, you know. It just had a thing in the paper about that recently, where that Lucas guy confessed to a bunch of stuff he didn't do, you know. And we later on found out he didn't do it," said the juror.

Even though the juror had heard about Kathy's case, he convinced both the state and the defense that he could be an impartial juror, so he stayed in the jury pool.

After the state and the defense completed their questioning, several people were dismissed from the jury pool including a police officer and a sheriff's officer. Six jurors were finally selected with one alternate. The clerk gave the oath to the jury and read the bill of information, which stated that charges were made for simple burglary on or about September 8, 2004, when the defendant willfully and unlawfully committed simple burglary of a 1991 Ford Explorer. After reading the bill the judge dismissed the jury and asked that they return at 8:55 the next morning.

He reminded them to refrain from any reading of the newspaper or viewing the media as to avoid any kind of reference to the case.

❧

The wheels of justice were moving, but it seemed like they were moving at carriage speed. I wanted the trial to be over and the verdict to be read. I wanted him to be sentenced so I would know for at least a little while he would not be capable of committing any more crimes or causing any more pain to others. I knew Mr. Jones and Mr. Sylvester were working diligently to see justice prevail, but it seemed like the world around me had begun to spin in slow motion.

❧

Court was reconvened the next day, July 17, 2007.

The judge called everyone to order and said, "Okay. Good morning, everybody. What do we have to do first before we get cranked up with this trial?"

"Judge, I have both my witnesses here," said Mr. Sylvester.

The judge addressed the two witnesses, "The defense has moved to sequester the witnesses. Both of you have to remain outside the courtroom during the course of the entire trial. You are not to discuss your testimony or any aspect of this case with anyone, each other or anyone else, except perhaps the attorneys in this matter. So if you'll leave the courtroom, but remain near the courtroom, we'll call you back when your presence is needed."

After both witnesses left the courtroom, Mr. Sylvester began his opening statement. He reminded the jurors that the defendant was charged with simple burglary and that the state had the burden to prove beyond a reasonable doubt that he was guilty of the crime. He recounted the details of September 8, 2004, when the burglary took place. He explained that the owner of the 1991 Ford Explorer had just come home that evening from his second job.

With a smile on his face he said, "Notice what I said. He had just come home from his second job. Some people realize that one job is not enough if you want to have a certain standard in the way you live. And when you have people of that stature, they work hard for things that they get. He parked his car under his carport and went in the house. The next morning when he got up to go to his first job, he noticed someone in his vehicle. The man sitting in the defendant's chair was asleep in the driver's side of his vehicle."

He went on to say that the police were called and two deputies answered the call.

"They noticed the back rear window on the passenger side had been busted out, where the defendant gained entry into the vehicle. When the defendant was searched they found a bottle of cologne in his pocket. The owner of the vehicle told officers that the cologne belonged to him. A black bag was found on the floorboard which contained assorted change, a black skull cap, and a pair of bolt cutters. The owner of the vehicle said the change was the only item in the bag that belonged to him."

Mr. Sylvester wanted the jury to understand fully what the law stated about intent so he explained to them, "Intent is discerned by the actions of the individual once they enter a place or do something. The defendant broke out the window, and once inside, rummaged through the vehicle, took change out of the console, put it in his black bag that contained a black skull cap and the bolt cutters. Then he took a bottle of cologne that belonged to the victim and put it in his pocket and fell asleep. It's kind of like Goldie Locks, except this was the baby bear's chair and that's where he was—unauthorized entry into a vehicle with the intent to commit a theft. That's what we're going to show you in this trial."

Mr. Thomas asked to briefly speak. "Mr. Sylvester has laid out most of the facts of the case to you. The important part that you're going to have to resolve for yourself is this: "What was the defendant's intent in the vehicle? He fell asleep. They woke him up in the morning. The police took him out while he was asleep. The question you really have to resolve is whether or not the state can prove through circumstantial evidence that excludes every reasonable hypothesis of innocence that the defendant intended to commit a theft inside that vehicle."

After opening statements, the state called the owner of the vehicle as the first witness. His testimony was that he had arrived home from work around 9:30 or 10:00 p.m. and pulled his vehicle under the carport and locked all the doors. He explained that when he went outside the next morning to go to work, he saw the defendant in the vehicle asleep, so he called the police. He went on to tell the jury that he watched as the police searched the defendant and found his cologne in the defendant's pocket. He also noticed all of his change was missing from the console area.

When Mr. Thomas had a chance to cross examine the owner of the vehicle he said, "I just have a couple of questions for you. When you locked your vehicle that night, did you stay at the house?

"Yes, sir," said the witness.

"You went to sleep?"

"Yes, sir, I did."

"Did you hear any noise?" asked the defendant's lawyer.

"No, sir."

"Was the vehicle near where you sleep?"

"No, sir. It was under my carport. My room is in the rear of the house, the very back."

After several other questions, the first witness was excused, and Mr. Sylvester called the officer who worked the robbery to the stand. After the same line of questioning, he asked one last question. "Do you recognize the man who was in the vehicle that day?"

The witness pointed to the defendant and said, "Yes, the gentleman on the far end of the table wearing the blue jumpsuit."

"When he got out of the vehicle and you secured him in handcuffs, did you find anything on his person?"

"Yes, a bottle of cologne."

"Did you show that bottle of cologne to the person that owned the vehicle and did he identify it as being his own?"

"Yes, then we gave the bottle of cologne back to the owner."

"I'd like to show you some items and tell me if you've ever seen them before."

"Yes, I've seen the duffle bag and the items inside—the bolt cutters, and the black knit cap."

At that time the state introduced into evidence the bag, the bolt cutters and a black knit hat. The last piece of evidence admitted was an envelope with some pocket change.

The last witness called for the day was the evidence officer. She identified the black bag and its contents and explained that the black bag and its contents were sealed since the date of the arrest.

After questioning the evidence officer, the state rested its case.

The judge addressed the jury, "All right. Ladies and gentlemen, you've heard all the evidence the state intends to present to support its case." Then he looked at the defense lawyer and asked, "What's next?"

Mr. Thomas replied, "The Defense rests also, Your Honor."

Turning to the jury, the judge said, "All right. That's all the evidence you're going to hear on this case. We're going to give you a chance to look at the evidence that's been presented to you. And then you'll hear the closing arguments in this case."

Mr. Sylvester paced back and forth in front of the jury as he delivered his first closing argument knowing in the back of his mind the importance of the outcome of the case. He reminded the jury of the definition of burglary and explained once more how the defendant burst out the window of the vehicle.

"He got fifty-eight cents and a bottle of cologne. The burglary was complete. He stole cologne. He stole change. He took it upon himself to damage property with the unauthorized entry and then to steal from a man he did not even know. So how is it you can in your wildest imagination come up with the conclusion that he didn't intend to permanently deprive him of the things that he took? It's simple burglary committed by the defendant."

After the state's closing arguments, Mr. Thomas stood up and faced the jury. "I want to thank you for your attention during this trial. The issue here is the intent. You've got a guy that crawls in the truck. He broke a forty dollar window. They did find him in the truck. Nobody is contesting that. The question is: What happens when the guy wakes up on his own, finds out where he is because he says he doesn't really know where he is because he had been drinking? He could just as easily have put the cologne back and gone on about his business. The state did not show you that the defendant intended to deprive the owner of the vehicle anything permanently. I would submit to you that in this case the state has not proven its position beyond a reasonable doubt and you should find the defendant not guilty of burglary."

Mr. Sylvester made one final argument: "This is not a fairytale. If you remember, I made mention of Goldie Locks earlier in this trial and the three bears. She goes to the house. She sits in the first—I'm not sure how it goes. But she ends up eating the porridge and breaking the baby bear's chair and then sleeping in the baby bear's bed. This is not Goldie Locks, you all. This is simple burglary. And I can't reiterate enough, it's simply that. The elements of the crime have been proven to you beyond a reasonable doubt. Find him guilty. Thank you."

The judge gave the jury their final instructions and the jury retired to the deliberation room at 11:41 a.m.

∾

The wheels of justice began spinning more quickly. After only fifty-nine minutes of deliberation, the jury returned to the courtroom at 12:40 p.m.

❦

After everyone was seated the judge asked the bailiff to hand him the verdict.

"Publish the verdict, please."

The clerk stood, "Guilty of simple burglary, dated July 17, 2007. Ladies and gentlemen of the jury, is this your verdict?"

The foreman of the jury answered, "Yes, your Honor; it is."

Mr. Thomas asked for the jury to be polled. Pieces of paper were given to each member of the jury to check yes or no. After reviewing all six of the jurors' verdicts, the judge declared, "The polling has just confirmed the announced verdict, and the defendant is found guilty based on the jury's verdict. The judge declared, "Sentencing will be set for 1:30 on Thursday, July 19."

❦

It was our first legal victory! With this conviction, he would have to spend at least some time in jail. This man had spent a life time of evading long-term sentences, but we were praying this time he wouldn't be so lucky.

❧

On the day of sentencing the judge said, "The sheer number of offenses in this man's past indicates he consistently breaks the law, and he is not going to stop. So, that justifies the maximum sentence imposed for simple burglary, twelve years."

After the sentencing, Mr. Sylvester quickly stood up and addressed the judge, "Your Honor, the state has filed a habitual bill of information charging him as a four felony offender. If the defendant's offenses meet all the requirements of the habitual offender law, he should be sentenced to life in prison without any possibility of parole. The judge then set a hearing date for September 25, 2007, to hear arguments on the matter.

❧

My family realized that the habitual offender hearing would be the most important day of our lives. It was the day we had worked for since I climbed those stairs and pushed aside the painful memories to begin our search for justice. It would either be a day of deliverance from the past or a day of complete devastation knowing that Kathy's killer would be walking the streets again one day. Either way, we knew that God would be with us no matter what the outcome of the hearing would be. That was our comfort. That had always been our comfort, even when Kathy was stolen from our lives.

❧

When the day of the hearing finally arrived, the defendant had retained a new lawyer, Mr. Hester, who immediately questioned what Mr. Jones' policy was for filing a habitual offender bill. "Does it have anything to do with this individual being a suspect in a murder case?"

Mr. Sylvester said, "The state respectfully refuses to answer as it has no relevance in this proceeding. The defendant has five prior felonies, not including the felony he was convicted of on the simple burglary."

The judge heard arguments from Mr. Hester concerning Mr. Jones' reasoning behind pursuing the habitual offender case. Because the defendant had changed lawyers since the simple burglary charge, the judge told him that after the state presented their case that day, Mr. Hester would be given some additional time to prepare arguments. Then the judge asked the state to go ahead and present its case.

Mr. Sylvester asked the judge for permission to get a fingerprint from the defendant. An identification officer took his fingerprint, and she was called as the state's first witness. The witness submitted copies of the fingerprints for the defendant's five prior felonies. One by one the fingerprint expert compared the fingerprints of the defendant's prior felonies with the prints she had just taken in the court room, and they were all matches.

After hearing all the felony charges brought against the defendant, the judge told the court, "If the evidence were concluded today, I would be compelled to find that the state has made its case; but because of the seriousness of this matter, the court will reconvene at a later date to make a decision."

Our emotions were stretched to the limit as the reconvening of the hearing was delayed time and time again. Finally, on January 22, 2008, the day we had long anticipated arrived.

∽

Mr. Hester began the hearing by delivering his argument to the judge.

"We believe and therefore allege that the habitual offender proceeding is being instituted because of the defendant's suspicion in a homicide matter. And we further believe that he is being treated differently than others criminally situated. We desire a hearing on the matter. We asked Mr. Jones to describe his policy for filing multiple offender bills, and he responded in writing saying each case is decided on its own merits."

Mr. Sylvester explained, "Throughout this prosecution, the only thing this man has been prosecuted for is a simple burglary. His past criminal history is the only basis for the habitual offender charge. Now, regardless of what else may be there, it's not being alleged by the state; it's being alleged by the defense. And it has no merit of what we're dealing with here. Because of what the statute says this man should be sentenced as a habitual offender. And the statute says he should be sentenced to life."

The judge explained to the defense, "Even if the district attorney put on a special effort regarding this individual because they thought he was a murderer, the constitution of the state of Louisiana allows the district attorney to make this decision. The law is very clear. The statutory law for this decision lies with the district attorney to either prosecute or not prosecute. Now what is left to do in this case?"

Mr. Sylvester quickly spoke up, "Sentence the defendant, your Honor."

Looking at the defendant, the judge said, "You are remanded to the custody of the state of Louisiana where you shall be imprisoned for the remainder of your natural life without benefit of parole, probation or suspension of sentence. That's all."

༄

And that was all! That was all my family wanted. We wanted justice for Kathy, and we finally had it!

༄

After the trial, the media asked Mr. Jones if the charges had been drummed up because the defendant was a suspected killer.

He replied, "Did we get a suspected serial killer off the street for stealing a bottle of cologne? Yes. Was it the right thing to do? Yes. But that's not the only reason he is serving life. His prior record supports this."

"Were you influenced at all by the cold case and the DNA evidence linked to the defendant?" another reporter asked.

Mr. Sylvester replied, "The district attorney told me to try the case. He didn't tell me why—I just tried the case—which, with his criminal history led to a life sentence."

⁓

Almost twenty-seven years after Kathy's death, on January 22, 2008, her murderer was sentenced to life in prison when he was convicted as a habitual offender. Over the years, I had imagined many different scenarios of how Kathy's murderer would be caught; but I can honestly say, I never dreamed my family and I would have played such a significant part in catching and bringing her killer to justice. I don't think I could have ever imagined in a million years a scenario like the one that actually unfolded. A bottle of sweet smelling cologne and some pocket change sent my sister's killer to prison for life! How sweet the scent of justice!

❧ *Chapter 15* ❧

....

A Face to Forgive

Since the man I believe murdered my sister was sent to prison, I'm often asked, "Are you mad at God because he was never officially charged with her murder—that he was never brought to trial for what he did to Kathy?"

My answer is always the same. God's plan might have been a little different than my plan; my plan involved charges being brought against him with a jury of his peers convicting him of rape and murder. It included going to court every day during the trial to see if I could understand why he had done something so cruel and heartless.

God's plan was very different than mine. While it involved putting a face to my sister's killer, His plan also included sparing us from the pain of reliving the difficult details of that horrible night during a media-centered trial. *His plan was best!*

∞

My job today involves inducting new teachers into the teaching profession and providing professional development for them so they'll be successful in the classroom. When we discuss testing students, I remind them that the purpose of a test it is to reveal how much their students have actually learned about a subject they have been taught and to assess how much growth they have made over time.

When I look at the trials we've experienced since Kathy was killed and during the whole process of bringing her killer to justice, I think of them as a self-assessment of my faith. The way I handle my trials when I am tested will reveal to me how much I've grown spiritually. God already knew how I would respond to every trial that came my way. I believe He wanted me to know how I would react to them, too.

During Kathy's visitation hours the day before the funeral, I watched Daddy take his test of faith. As logical as he was, I'm sure he found no logic in what happened to his first-born child. When we entered the dark, depressing room, Daddy got on his knees in front of Kathy's casket; instead of cursing God because He allowed her to be raped and killed, he said, "Thank you, God, for the time we had with her and the blessing she was to our lives."

In my assessment, Daddy passed his test of faith. His words revealed what he truly believed from studying God's Word, and it revealed how much faith he had in the God he loved. Through his example, Daddy reminded all of us, as we stood around her casket, that we should constantly draw our strength from God.

∽

In my Christian life, I've wandered through many deep valleys and planted my flag on many mountaintops. But only after meandering through the valleys have I realized how real God has become to me; I know without a doubt that I can't reach the top of the mountain without Him.

I know my trials are not unforeseen incidents. They are simply cuts to God's diamond in the rough. Whatever I go through in this life, however deep the cuts might get, I know God hasn't forgotten me. Just like light shines so gloriously through a diamond after it has been cut with precision, God reveals Himself to others through me, so they will look at me and wonder, "How does she have such peace after all she's lost?"

In every valley, with every painful cut, He has given me the peace that passes all understanding, mentioned in Philippians 4:6-7: "Don't worry about anything; instead, pray about everything; tell God your needs and don't forget to thank Him for His answers. If you do this you will experience God's peace, which is far more wonderful than the human mind can understand. His peace will keep your thoughts and your hearts quiet and at rest as you trust in Christ Jesus."

૭

When my daughter, Brittany, was a little girl, she was diagnosed with a growth problem, so I had to give her growth hormone shots every day for several years to help her gain more height. I cringed every time I poked that needle into her leg. It hurt my heart knowing that I was causing my own child pain, but she always reminded me, "No pain, no gain Mom!" Over time, the shots helped her gain two inches in height.

I'm sure God hurts when we experience the pain of death and other trials, just like I hurt for Brittany. In all truth, I would never take back any of the trials that have occurred since Kathy's death because with them came tremendous spiritual growth.

It says in Romans 5:3-5: "We can rejoice, too, when we run into problems and trials for we know that they are good for us – they help us learn to be patient. And patience develops strength of character in us and helps us trust God more each time we use it until finally our hope and faith are strong and steady. Then, when that happens, we are able to hold our heads high no matter what happens and know that all is well, for we know how dearly God loves us, and we feel this warm love everywhere within us because God has given us the Holy Spirit to fill our hearts with His love."

There's no doubt in my mind that the deep cut in 1981, and every incision since then, especially during my quest for justice, has increased my patience and trust in God that He has a plan and that He hears my prayers and cares deeply about them, especially when I am fulfilling His desires.

God put the desire in my heart to bring my sister's killer to justice, and I accepted the task before me. Why now and not twenty-five years ago? I don't know, but God does, and at every step of the journey He kept His promises:

> Psalm 55:22: "Give your burdens to the Lord. He will carry them."
> *He carried my burdens at every dead end.*
> Psalm 9:9: "All who are oppressed may come to Him. He is a refuge for them in their times of trouble."
> *He was my refuge in every moment of despair.*
> Romans 8:28 (KJV): "And we know that all things work together for good to them that love God, to them who are called according to His purpose."
> *He turned tragedy into justice for all.*
> Philippians 4:13 (KJV): "I can do all things through Christ who strengthens me."
> *He strengthened me with His words and His peace when I didn't think I could continue the task before me.*

Kathy's killer will more than likely never be brought to trial for her murder, but we know without a doubt who her murderer is—where he is—and most importantly, we know God's judgment will be sufficient. But there was one thing He required of us—to forgive him.

How can we not forgive him? Christ forgives us daily for all of our sins, and He expects us to forgive others. Matthew 6:14-15 says, "If you forgive those who sin against you, your heavenly Father will forgive you. But if you refuse to forgive others, your Father will not forgive your sins."

Justice is as sweet-smelling as the cologne that sent her killer to prison for life, but forgiveness is an even sweeter scent. Another reason God allowed us to find Kathy's killer after all those years is because we needed to stop hiding and forgive; it's hard to forgive an unknown person—a person without a face.

❧ *Chapter 16* ❧

....

Forgiving a Killer

From the very beginning of the journey I began in October of 2003, I kept all of my notes about Kathy's case in the bottom drawer of my dresser. Old newspaper clippings, photographs, copies of Kathy's diary, and pages of notes I had written as I searched for answers were all packed away in that drawer.

Even after the life-sentence, I still collected articles and filed them away in that same drawer. From time to time since then, I still looked in that crowded drawer, took out the old articles, and read them. One article from a local paper stood out. It was the article that contained the picture of our family standing around Kathy's gravestone with the cross in the background.

I read the article over and over again, especially the excerpts from our press conference statement, expressing how we had chosen to forgive Kathy's killer:

For twenty-six years we have been waiting for the day the justice process would begin for Kathy. We have always known that if justice didn't take place for her killer while he was on the earth, it would take place after his death. We are so thankful that we will be able to see that process begin now.

Please pray for our family as we begin this long journey. It will not be an easy one, but we will gladly experience personal pain if it means bringing justice to Kathy. Please pray for him as well. We have forgiven this man for what he did to our family because forgiveness frees us. Hate would just keep us chained down, but we do believe that he needs to pay for the crime that he committed so long ago.

I couldn't get that one word out of my mind—"forgiven."

I asked myself if I had really forgiven him or if those were just words—empty words that I said that day. How could I know for certain I had truly forgiven him? The only way I knew to find the answer was to pray, "God, I need you to show me whether or not I have true forgiveness in my heart. Please make the answer clear to me."

One Sunday morning as we arrived home after church services, I placed my Bible on top of several others on the bottom shelf of a small wooden table, just like I did every Sunday. As I watched the Bible slide into its place, a thought suddenly entered my mind, and a smile emerged. God had spoken to me, and I knew exactly what I had to do.

I picked up one of my Bibles that was on the bottom of the stack, took it to my bedroom, and closed the door behind me. I wanted Kathy's killer to know that when God sent His Son, Jesus, to die for my sins, He also died for the sins of the man sitting in a jail cell who had committed murder. I began highlighting verses in the Bible that spoke of forgiveness and God's love. I marked scripture that would show him his need for Christ. Then, I opened the Bible to the front inside cover and wrote these words:

> *I want you to know I have forgiven you; but more importantly, God will forgive you. If you will confess your sins and ask Him to forgive you, He is faithful and just and will cleanse you from all unrighteousness. I have highlighted and marked several verses for you to read.*

I felt such relief after writing those words. I closed the Bible and gently placed it in the dresser drawer on top of all the files I had collected over the years. It sat there for months, and every time I saw it, making no move to send it to him, I wondered, *Are my words just words?—empty words?*

A few weeks later, getting ready to go to work, I finally felt led to go to that bottom dresser drawer. I picked up the Bible and asked God to give me the strength I would need to do what I was about to do. I knew it was time to completely let go of my past. I got on the Internet and found the address of the prison. I put the Bible in my car on the seat beside me. During my lunch hour, I drove across town to the post office.

When I pulled up in front of the post office and got out of the car, I had the same nervous feeling as the day I pulled into the parking lot at the school where I met the retired detective, Ray Vail. Once again, I was not going to let my nerves stop me from doing what I knew I needed to do. I walked up the stairs of the building and with my hands shaking slightly, I opened the door.

In the entranceway I found the packaging material I needed to send my gift of forgiveness. I paused to gain control of my hands and slipped the Bible inside a small box, sealed it with tape, and wrote Kathy's killer's name and the prison address on the outside of the package.

I stood in line for what seemed to be an eternity. When I handed the package to the woman behind the counter, I asked her how much money I owed for postage. When she said, "$4.65," I thought, *How cheap the price to pay for what might help save someone's soul*!

I handed the postal worker my money; she smiled and said, "Have a good day." If she only knew what an understatement that was!

The freedom I felt when I released the package into her hands is almost indescribable. It's the type of freedom you feel when you've been weighted down with a heavy load and someone finally comes along and takes your burden and places it on their back. I felt a new sense of freedom, just like a prisoner feels after being released from his shackles. God had lifted the burden of hate I didn't even realize had been hidden and tucked away in my heart for so many years.

To this day, I don't know if the man we believe to be Kathy's killer has read any of the words I marked for him in the Bible, but I do know that sending him my Bible was the last step I needed to take in the process of forgiveness to be free from the past. The faith that allowed Daddy to drop to his knees at the funeral home in thanksgiving of Kathy's short life on earth, and the faith that helped my mother survive her battles with cancer was the same faith that gave me the strength to forgive a killer.

It says in Isaiah 55:10-11, "As the rain and snow come down from heaven and stay upon the ground to water the earth, and cause the grain to grow and to produce seed for the farmer and bread for the hungry, so also is my Word. I send it out and it always produces fruit. It shall accomplish all I want it to, and prosper everywhere I send it."

God's Word has been sent out, and now it is up to the man who is sitting in jail for being convicted of stealing a bottle of cologne and pocket change to decide if he wants to experience the sweet scent of forgiveness in his own life.

❧ *Chapter 17* ❧

A Story to Tell

Almost twenty-nine years after my sister was killed, I began to have another strong desire that I felt came from God. This time the desire in my heart was to share my family's story.

I don't profess to be a writer, so time and time again, I tried to push those feelings to the side and just ignore them like I tried to ignore the fact that I had an English term paper due during the last month of my senior year of high school.

No matter how hard I tried to suppress those feelings, the need to put my story into words just wouldn't go away. The need grew to be as strong as the desire I had the year before I turned forty to discover the truth that was hidden under a dark cloud of distress.

This time I needed to open up what was in my heart and share some of my deepest and most personal thoughts. There is not a doubt in my mind that the desire I had in my heart then and now, came from God.

Why would God give me the desire to expose not only my life but Kathy's life in this way? My sister was a wonderful Christian girl with a very strong faith, and I knew she would want her story told if there was only a slight chance that just one person might be touched by it in a way that would bring him or her closer to God or to a personal relationship with Christ, even if that one person was her own killer.

The desire to share my story also grew because I wanted my two daughters to know as they live out their Christian lives, they can talk about their faith to others, but their real voices will be heard the loudest through the actions they take. Words can't show someone what is in your heart, but actions can. That's why they need to know my story, and why they need to know the reason I sent my Bible to their Aunt Kathy's killer.

Many people commented after Kathy's death that she was just in the wrong place at the wrong time. It's true if she had not gone to the college club, and if she had not been out on the road so late, the whole, horrible nightmare would have never happened.

The fact is that she was on the road in front of the college that fateful night in 1981, and all of the tragic events I have written about really did happen. I don't know why she had to die in such a cruel and evil way, but I do know it was allowed to happen by God, just as He allowed His own Son to suffer and be placed on a cruel cross.

I have to believe God will allow something good to come out of her suffering, just as He allowed Christ's suffering for the good of humanity. God has promised this in His Word when He said, "We know that all things work together for good to them that love God, to them who are the called according to his purpose" (romans 8:28 KJV).

I know in my own life that my personal faith in Him was strengthened through it all, and through my suffering I was reminded that the things of this earth are only temporary, but the things of God are eternal.

Just as I knew God led me down the path to help catch Kathy's killer, I knew He led me down the path to write Kathy's story. I knew He would help me every step of the way just as he had in the past.

As I tried to write the last chapter of my book though, I had a very difficult time finding the right ending to my story. I prayed and asked God to give me the final words that He would have me to write. Then I realized why the words wouldn't come to me: It's because the story isn't over—at least I hope it isn't over.

With all my heart I hope one day Kathy's killer will decide to open up the Bible I sent him and read it. My prayer is that when he reads it, he will also see the need to release his burdens to the Lord and ask for forgiveness that would give him freedom. Not freedom from the punishment he will have to face on this earth, but freedom from the consequences of a life without the assurance of salvation through Jesus Christ. It is my prayer he will write the final chapter of my story, and I pray that it will have a happy ending.

Acknowledgments

When I finished writing the words God had placed on my heart, I realized there were so many wonderful people I needed to thank for being a part of Kathy's life or for helping me through the process of telling my story.

To my editor, Edie, there is no doubt God sent you my way to help me put the final touches on my manuscript. God used your wonderful talents to help me tell my story. For this I thank you.

Lisa, thank you for your wonderful designs and encouraging words when I needed them the most.

Thank you, Brian, for being so special to Kathy. She loved you dearly and enjoyed all the time you spent together. Your sister had to search for you while you camped out in the woods that weekend to tell you about her tragic death. I'm sorry you had to find out that way. I want you to know Kathy mentioned in an autobiography she wrote a few months before her death how close the two of you had become. She loved you very much.

Bruce, I know you were so protective of Kathy. As I was doing research for my book, I found out you followed her half way to her destination the night before she was killed. I wasn't surprised at all when I found out that information because you were always so thoughtful and kind. I know as you flashed your lights at her to tell her bye that evening, you had no idea it would be your last goodbye. Thank you for sharing such special memories with my family.

Butch, we have lost touch over the years, but you brought the laughter that helped all of us make it through those dark days. God has given you the gift of encouragement, and in those days he gave you an extra dose of it to pour out on my family. I am so grateful to you for that.

Kathy, you know how much my sister loved you. Thank you for being one of her best friends and for being so close to her during her final years with us. You brought so much joy to her life.

Karen, you were Kathy's friend, but you were Amy's best friend. Thank you for becoming another sister to both of us during the years after her death. You helped fill the giant void Kathy's death had created in our lives. We knew we could never replace Kathy, but your sweet spirit was exactly what our family needed during that time.

Carol, you had already moved away to college when Kathy was killed, but I know you were deeply affected by her death. You were Kathy's best friend for her entire life. There are so many memories, but my fondest memories are of the times we sang *Those Were the Days* in harmony together as we sat on Mamaw's porch swing. Thank you for being her best friend for all those years and for loving her dearly.

Lori, thank you is not enough to say to my best friend. You have known me my entire life, and I don't know what I would do without our friendship. Kathy's death was just the first of many tragedies we would experience together, but our faith and our friendship have grown through each and every experience. I know from my own experience that God puts special people in our lives, and I am so thankful you were chosen to be that special person in my life.

To all of Kathy's friends who were members of the Greenacres youth group, thank you for helping make such beautiful memories with Kathy over the years. Traveling and singing with Bro. Bob and Mrs. Johnye were such amazing and fun times. So much of Kathy's growth as a Christian occurred during those precious years.

Hal, Charlie and Nancy, you sacrificed so much of your time to spend with our youth group. Thank you for helping all of the youth at Greenacres Baptist Church grow in our Christian faith. Hal, you taught us how to sing in four part harmony and helped us develop the talents God had given us. Charlie and Nancy, I'll never forget our youth trip to Eureka Springs to see the Passion Play or the trip to Biloxi where we had the Lord's Supper on the beach. All three of you were such an important part of Kathy's life.

Dr. Adkins and Mrs. Martha Sue, thank you for being my parents' best friends and staying so close to our family during those difficult days. Thank you, Dr. Adkins, for being there for my daddy and for being like a second father to me after Daddy passed away.

I would be remiss if I didn't thank the congregation of Greenacres Baptist Church for being our pillar of support for so many years. Kathy's Christian foundation was built by those at Greenacres who were willing to devote their time to teaching God's truths to her. God provided us with a wonderful church family that helped support us during that awful, dark time of our lives.

Rebecca, when your family moved into the house across the street, I can remember how excited Kathy was to find out there was a girl in the new family who was close to her age. Kathy got so close to you over the years, and I'm thankful you were her friend. Thank you for encouraging me when you found out I was researching Kathy's cold case.

The Wilsons, my second family, thank you for helping me through each day after Kathy's death by giving me your unconditional love and support. I'm so glad to be part of such a loving and caring family.

The Carney family, Defee family, Whorton family, and Wooden family, thank you for your love and support throughout the years. Family was so important to Kathy, and she loved all of her uncles, aunts, and cousins dearly.

Mama, I love you. Thank you for showing me how to be strong in my faith. I saw you pick yourself up and continue to live for the Lord after losing your daughter. I saw the same courage and strength as you fought two battles with cancer and after losing your parents, and your husband and best friend. Thank you for allowing me to write this book even though I know it was painful for you to have to remember the past. Thank you for being the best Christian example and best parent I could ever dream of having.

Amy, you were just a young teenager when Kathy died, and the four year span between our ages seemed like a huge gulf separating our lives. After her death, that age span seemed to disappear, and our relationship began to grow and has not stopped growing even to this day. You are the most kind and caring person I've ever known. Your heart is bigger than the ocean itself, and you remind me so much of Kathy in that respect. I'm so thankful to have you as a sister.

Steve, you were just a little boy when Kathy died, but your words the day of her death were full of wisdom beyond your years. You reminded us she was in a better place, in heaven, with Jesus. I'm so thankful you came to know Jesus too, many years after Kathy went to be with Him. I'm thankful I can see a little bit of Daddy every day just by watching and listening to my little brother. I'm glad God placed that same desire in your heart to find out what happened to Kathy. Thank you for being such a wonderful brother.

Kim, we are so blessed to have you in our family. Thank you for always saying yes when I asked you to help me with the editing process of my book. You are a wonderful sister-in-law, and I'm thankful God added you to our family.

Sonny, thank you for putting up with late night phone calls when I needed Amy to help me with my manuscript. I also appreciate you being there for Amy as we searched for justice for Kathy. God knew what He was doing when He put you and my sister together.

Thank you, Brittany and Katelyn, for having to watch your mama cry so many tears as I worked to complete this book. I'm so thankful both of you have repented of your sins and asked Jesus into your lives to be your personal Lord and Savior. I love watching you grow every day in the Lord. Always remember to stay close to Him, and when you are in the valleys of your life, He will be there with you. I love both of you with all my heart.

Todd, you stood by my side through that terrible time in 1981, and you have been standing by my side ever since. You are the man God chose for me, and I'm so grateful to you for loving me. God was in the center of our relationship then just like He is today. Thank you for supporting me and always encouraging me. You are not just my husband. You are my best friend.

Picture taken a few months before Kathy's death in 1981

(My high school sweet heart, husband, and best friend)

Pictures and Memories from the Past

(This picture of Kathy was taken just a few months before her death.)

(Kathy's high school graduation picture)

(Kathy and me)
(Left to right: Debbie and Kathy)

(Kathy and me)
(Left to right: Kathy and Debbie)

(Kathy and me)
(Left to right: Kathy and Debbie)

(Kathy and me)
(Left to right: Debbie and Kathy)

(Left to right: Debbie, Mama, Daddy, and Kathy)

(Kathy and me)
(Left to right: Kathy and Debbie)

(Left to right: Debbie, Mamaw and Amy, Papaw and Steve, and Kathy)

(Rebecca and Kathy)

Picture of our church youth group as we traveled and sang together

(Front row: Debbie, Lori, Carol, Kathy, and Vicki)
(Middle row: Kathy, Bronna, Tonya, and Veronica)
(Back row: Tara, Jan, Joan, and Tollisa)

Picture of youth girls on one of our singing trips
(Left to right: Lori, Vicki, and Kathy)

Youth trip to Eureka Springs, Arkansas

(Front row/Left to right – Kathy, Carol, Lori, and Charlie)
(Back row/Left to right – Terry, Hal, Debbie Kathy, and Todd)

(Brian and Kathy)

(Bruce and Kathy)

(Butch and Kathy)

(Church Youth Group – picture taken several months after Kathy's death)

Front row: Debbie, Lori, Hal, and Brian
Back row: Bruce, Butch, Kathy, Karen and Amy

The Best Policy
By Kathy

God offers an insurance plan
And with His lifetime policy
You can't go wrong

He guides you with His hand
As no other person can
And if you follow Him
He'll never let you down

He's there to protect you
When the going gets rough
And He's never going to leave you
He'll just stick by your side

You never have to worry
About your future life
Because you know what's in store for you
Is really out of sight

God's insurance plan protects you
Better than the rest
You'll have the shield
You'll have the rock
And you'll have Eternal Life!

Christmas

By Kathy

As the fire flickers in front of me
I reminisce on Christmas past
My thoughts return to yesterday's world
Blocking out thoughts of today

In this foreign Christmas of days long ago
There is a scene before me of a small child
Being lain in a manger by His mother
And a star shining brightly above

Three men approach the babe with gifts
Of foreign spices and gold
And as they look upon the child
They bow and humbly behold him

There is no doubt in their minds
That He is truly a special child
And if you listen close there is a mysterious song
Ringing in men's hearts
Beholding this small child whom they knew
Would someday change men's lives
They knew then as we do today

That He is the son of God

As my thoughts are recoiled to the present world
I can see things in a different light
That babe is not dead, but alive today
And He lives within my heart

Things seem much clearer now
When you turn back to long ago
And base your thoughts on Him today
And wish Him a Happy Birthday!

Answers from the Author

Why did you write your book?

Several years after the final events in my book took place, I began to feel God's calling to tell my story. I'm a very private person, so this was a calling I tried to ignore for some time. I knew I would have to write about some of my most private thoughts and feelings, and I just didn't know if I could do that. I was also scared to death to write a book because that's not something I had ever aspired to do! When I finally gave in to His call, He began giving me the words to write. It was therapy for me, and I am praying someone will be touched by reading *Sweet Scent of Justice*.

How did you know God wanted you to tell your story?

That's an easy question to answer! He wouldn't let me rest until I placed that final punctuation mark on the final sentence in the book. At night I would pray for God to give me the words to say because sometimes the words just wouldn't come to me. I kept a pen and notepad beside my bed, and time after time, I would wake up in the middle of the night with just the right words. God is so good, and He gave me strength to complete the task He asked me to do.

What is your favorite scripture verse?

I have many, but I love the scripture in Mark 5:25-34, "In the crowd was a woman who had been sick for twelve years with a hemorrhage. She had suffered much from many doctors through the years and had become poor from paying them, and was no better but, in fact, was worse. She had heard all about the wonderful miracles Jesus did, and that is why she came up behind him through the crowd and touched his clothes. For she thought to herself, 'If I can just touch his clothing, I will be healed.' And sure enough, as soon as she had touched him, the bleeding stopped and she knew she was well! Jesus realized at once that healing power had gone out from him, so he turned around in the crowd and asked, 'Who touched my clothes?' His disciples said to him, 'all this crowd pressing around you and you ask who touched you?' But he kept on looking around to see who it was who had done it. Then the frightened woman, trembling at the realization of what had happened to her, came and fell at his feet and told him what she had done. And he said to her, 'Daughter, your faith has made you well; go in peace, healed of your disease."

A few years ago, my doctor and several doctors from M.D. Anderson diagnosed me with kidney cancer. I had my right kidney removed, and miraculously it was NOT a malignant tumor. For several weeks while I waited on the pathology report, I read that scripture over and over, and I prayed I would have the same faith the woman in scripture had. God gave me a peace about it, and the doctors were shocked when the reports showed no cancer. I wasn't shocked at all, but I was VERY thankful! I could write another book about that whole experience!

How can I have faith in God?

There IS a God in Heaven and He loves you as you are. God's love is unconditional, and it is a gift for everyone who is willing to receive it. If you are willing to admit that you are a sinner, repent of your sins, and believe He died to save you from your sins, you can receive the free gift of salvation. You just need to call upon the name of the Lord and have faith He will save you, and then you can experience His love and forgiveness. At that point Christ will come into your life and fill the empty void that we all experience without Him.

Debbie Wilson has been an educator for over twenty-six years. She is currently serving as a New Teacher Induction Coordinator where she provides professional development to new teachers entering the teaching profession. She also teaches online classes at a local college where she received her undergraduate degree in Elementary Education, her Master's Degree in Elementary Education, and her certification in the area of Administration and Supervision. She has been married to Todd, her high school sweetheart, for twenty-seven years, and they have two beautiful daughters, Brittany and Katelyn. Debbie can be contacted at debbiewilson.org.

28302199R00121

Made in the USA
Lexington, KY
12 December 2013